Parachute Prayer

The Practice of Praying Continually

Janet Benlien Reeves

ISBN-13: 978-0692326435
ISBN-10: 069232643X

Cover art by rivka/Shutterstock.com

To Mike

Best friend – Boyfriend
Forever my love

I can't wait to see where the tricycle will take us next!

Contents

Introduction

History

While a teenager in high school, my middle son, Alex, started traveling down a troubled and painful road. His choices were breaking my heart, and thoughts about what he was doing nearly consumed my mind. When a child hurts, no matter what he's going through, his parents hurt too, and I was grieving all the time.

One day, I got in my truck to go pick up Alex and my younger son, Seth, from school. I turned on the radio and hit the seek button in hopes of finding something happy to listen to. I was surprised when a Christian song started playing. We'd been living in Middle-of-Nowhere, Texas for three months, and I'd never been able to find a Christian station. Just country—lots of country. So I was amazed to hear this song on what turned out to be a Christian station after all.

Even better though, the song was a then-new title by Paul Alan called *To Bring You Back*. I'd never heard this song before, but the words caught my attention right away. With tears in my eyes, I just sat there and listened to this beautiful song about all the lengths our Good Shepherd, Jesus, goes to in order to bring His lost sheep back into the fold. Then I prayed and praised my Lord for finding such a comforting way to let me know He cared about my son, He had the situation in hand, and He was working to bring Alex back.

From that day on, whenever I was driving in my truck, I was listening to that Christian station and praying along with one song after another that prompted me to pray for Alex and praise my loving God. The funny thing is, one month before we moved from that place, that radio station disappeared as mysteriously as it came. I was never able to find it again. I'll let you make of that what you will. I believe God worked a generous miracle to encourage a mother with a broken heart.

In any case, as I got into the habit of letting songs prompt me to pray, I started noticing that other things in my world were reminding me to pray as well. I began looking more intently for these, almost making a game of it, setting up prayer prompts for specific concerns. As I discovered their value in my life, I started blogging about them, figuring that others might be blessed by the practice, too. I called these prompts *Parachute Prayers*.

Concept

When I first started keeping a blog, my goal was to become more intentional about seeking, finding, and sharing the biblical truths God was teaching me. I wanted to help my readers do this, too! As I've explained it at *Wildflower Faith*, God plants life lessons everywhere, like wildflowers. We simply have to slow down and pay attention, so we won't just walk on by, leaving them unnoticed, unlearned, and untold — to wither and die unseen.

Prayer can work in much the same way. The reminders are all around us. Therefore, we can train ourselves, as I did while praying for Alex, to be more intentional about sending up prayers about anything and everything all the time. I think this is what Paul meant when he told us to "pray continually" (1 Thessalonians 5:17). Practicing the concept is a meaningful — and often fun — exercise.

As I started sharing these reminders on my blog, I wanted them to have a name my readers would recognize that would also fit my wildflower theme. Dandelions immediately came to mind. You pick a Dandelion, blow on it gently, and send the seeds flying through the air. Prayer is like that! You send your prayers to Heaven, and God just blesses everyone! You never know where the blessings will land—but God does. They aren't as random as they seem.

Interestingly enough, the fluffy, white things that carry Dandelion seeds wherever the wind blows are called parachutes. And that image fits the concept I'm trying to explain perfectly. A *Parachute Prayer* is one you whisper when an outside influence prompts you to release it, just like a breath of air prompts the Dandelion to release its parachutes.

Each *Parachute Prayer* idea included in this book is there to help us all remember to breathe those prayers more faithfully. Then, just as Dandelion parachutes carry seeds to help Dandelions grow in some of the most unlikely places, our prayers, by God's Spirit, can be used to build God's kingdom and help His people grow.

How to Use This Book

Though it would be possible for a person to sit down and read through this book fairly quickly, I'm hoping that you, dear reader, will savor it more slowly than that. Each *Parachute Prayer* is a habit to develop over time, a spiritual discipline to work at. Consider reading one a day, or maybe only one at the start of each week. Then give yourself time to practice. If you're trying to remember to pray about the music you hear on your radio, for example, focus on remembering to do that until you start to do this automatically, without reminding yourself. When you reach that point, you're ready to read the next *Parachute Prayer*.

When I shared some of these ideas with a friend, she said, "Janet, if I pray when I encounter all of those things, I'll be praying all the time!"

Good! That's the idea.

But don't let it overwhelm you. Practice one *Parachute Prayer* at a time, and soon you'll realize just how simple, yet meaningful, it is to talk to God continually — to talk to Him just as you breathe.

Father, thank You for scattering prayer prompts everywhere. They remind us of You. They remind us of needs. So please help us to notice them. Keep us mindful of moments in which we can offer prayers for the good of Your kingdom and the glory of Your name. We love You, Lord. Amen.

Praying at Home

Praying while Doing Housework

When my kids were little, we had a family chore that I dubbed, "General Pick-up." When I told the family we needed to do some general pick-up, they knew that a lot of our personal belongings had managed to wander from their places to clutter up the house. I expected everyone to pick up the things that were out of place, whether they were theirs or not, and put them away. It only took a few minutes, but what a difference it made!

Whether your family practices some form of "General Pick-up" or not, we all spend time each day on household upkeep and family care. Let's turn this time into an opportunity for *Parachute Prayer*. As we work with various items around our homes, let's pray for their owners. As we fold laundry, let's thank God for the ones who wear the clothes. As we dust or vacuum, let's pray for the person who lives in whatever room we're working in, about whatever we know he or she is probably doing at that time. As we cook, let's pray for the health of family members. As we pick up toys, let's pray that our children will always make wise and wholesome entertainment choices.

If we let Him, God's Spirit will lead us as we work to pray throughout the day for the people we love most. Let's have fun with this!

Father, as we handle the belongings of family members, moving every item into its place, remind us to use that time for prayer on their behalf. Amen.

Praying for People Who Come to the Door

When people come to your door or walk by your window, pray for them. God brought them to you — or into your sight, so send up a prayer on their behalf. Salespeople, the mail carrier, the utility meter checker, neighbors, kids selling cookies, and so on . . . all can benefit from a *Parachute Prayer*.

I'll never forget one young woman who came to my door. She was selling cleaning products — products I happen to be allergic to. Before I could tell her I wasn't interested, she started talking very quickly, giving me no time to politely interrupt. It was only when she raised the spray bottle, intending to clean something on my porch to show me how wonderful the product was that I held up a hand and calmly asked her to please not do that because the spray would make me sick. The woman did not take this news well, called me a liar, and threw a verbal temper tantrum all the way down my front walk.

I'll never know what was going on in this woman's life to cause her to react so aggressively, but when salespeople come to my door, I often remember her and send a prayer for her well-being God's way.

Thankfully, not all people who come to our doors are confrontative, yet all people do have needs for which we can pray. So when God brings people to our doors or past our windows, let's pray — for their salvation and strength to live God's way, for their health, for their families, for whatever comes to mind. God knows their needs and He's faithful. If we ask Him, He'll bless them indeed.

Father, please help us to answer our doors with smiles on our faces and prayers in our hearts. And as we'll sometimes pray for strangers we're meeting face to face, please help us discern the best way to pray. Please meet their greatest needs. Amen.

Praying for Kids We See Playing Outside

I especially love praying for children as I see them playing outside or walking home from school. I've been praying for children since I was in high school and met the cutest little two-year-old I'd ever seen. I knew more about her parents than a high school student probably should and realized that this precious child would *not* be raised in a Christian home. Someone had to lead her to Jesus! I don't know what's become of her, but still I pray. God put her on my heart that day.

Not only can we pray for the salvation of children but also that God will protect them as they grow into teenagers and young adults. Teens today live in a spiritual battle zone. Drugs and alcohol, sex before marriage, huffing, cutting, eating disorders, strange religions and anti-religions, so many ideas that run contrary to Scripture and a Christian worldview — the list is entirely too long! Even kids from Christian homes are struggling with the pressures they face — *so we must pray.*

If children are blessed with a genuine knowledge of Jesus at an early age, they'll not only receive salvation but also the strength to resist temptation to commit future sins. By choosing not to yield, they'll be spared from harsh consequences that can follow them through life. For the children of our neighborhoods, when we see them, let's pray.

Father, the children we see in our neighborhoods usually seem happy and carefree, but only You know what trials and temptations they will face as they grow. Remind us to pray for them often. We want them to grow up knowing You. Make a difference in their lives, Lord. Amen.

Praying for Our Spouses When They're Home and Away

When my husband is home, he leaves his keys, wallet, and phone together in a particular place. They're out of place, but not really. They're waiting for him; they're ready to go. And I like seeing them in their out-of-place place because their presence means my husband is home—unless he's left and forgotten part of his collection in which case I call him to let him know—unless the part he left behind just happens to be his phone. Then he's on his own.

Fortunately for Mike, the keeping-them-all-together strategy works pretty well. But that's not my topic for today. I've learned to turn these items into two prompts for *Parachute Prayer*.

First, when I see Mike's phone, wallet, and keys, I'm reminded to pray for him. I thank God for his life and for bringing him into mine. Then I ask God to watch over him and help him with whatever I know is on his mind. I also ask Him to provide for all of my husband's needs according to His wisdom—even for things that God sees coming, but Mike or I may not.

Second, when I notice the absence of these items during the day, I'm reminded to pray for my

14

husband at work. I ask God to give him wisdom, patience, endurance, tact, discipline, and whatever else comes to mind. God has a purpose for Mike and wants him to do well as he reaches out to others in Jesus' name. I want to see this happen, too!

If you aren't married, you can adapt this *Parachute Prayer* for parents or roommates. If you live alone, you'll be reminded to pray for yourself! (It is important to do this from time to time, too.) Just choose something that the one you plan to pray for leaves out when home but takes when on the go. When you notice its presence or absence, pause for a moment to pray.

Father, please help us notice often, so we'll remember to pray for these people each day. Amen.

Praying for Decision-Makers Whose Choices
Concern Us

It's easy to become alarmed when we read or hear in the news that a national or world leader or group of leaders is making decisions contrary to God's known will, in other words, in opposition to what's clear in His Word.

We don't have to be alarmed, though. Our sovereign God is in control. He knows what's going on, who's behind it, and how it will end. And nobody does anything without His consent. He may not approve, but He does allow, and when He does, He knows just what He's going to do about it.

So. No worries. God's got this.

In the meantime, though, there is something more positive than panic that we can do whenever we hear alarming news such as this. Like the writer of Psalm 138, we can pray. In fact, we can even pray that writer's words. Psalm 138:4-5 is a prayer for the leaders of this earth: "May all the kings of the earth praise you, Lord, when they hear what you have decreed. May they sing of the ways of the Lord, for the glory of the Lord is great." –Psalm 138:4-5

When God brings leaders to mind through any news source, let's pray, like the writer of Psalm 138, that they will all learn to praise Him. Let's pray they'll learn what God has decreed. Let's pray that they'll come to sing of His glory as they realize His glory is great.

In Romans 13:1, Paul tells us that "there is no authority except that which God has established." That being the case, those authorities need direction from God. I have no doubt that He can and will use them for His purposes right *where* they are right *as* they are, but just think how much more effective they'd be and how much more fulfilled personally if they were working in cooperation with God, living as His faithful servants, longing to touch His heart. Let's pray that God will draw them to Him and work to make this so.

Father, there is no authority except what You have established. Therefore, please remind us to pray for our leaders whether we agree with their actions or not. If they don't already, may they come to know, love, serve, and praise You. And if they do know You, Lord, please bless the work of their hands as they strive to do all for the glory of Your name. Amen.

Praying for People on Our Mind

We've lived in many places, and I remember people I've known in each. I've lost contact with some, of course, but they still come to mind from time to time. If something reminds me of our years in Colorado, I think of a particular group of friends. If I'm thinking of my hometown, I remember family and childhood friends.

These memories, triggered by whatever calls them to the front of my mind, are an opportunity for *Parachute Prayer*. The faces I picture may seem random, but I know it's possible God's reminding me of people because of their prayer needs.

You may not have moved often, but you probably have friends you've lost touch with over time: playmates from elementary school, college acquaintances, co-workers from a high school job, friends who have moved away.

When these people from the past make an appearance in our memories, let's pause for a moment to thank God that we know them and to ask Him to provide for all their needs.

Father, please bring memories of precious people to mind, people we've known in the past who need our prayers now. If they have particular needs You'd like us to cover, please guide our prayers in the right direction, whether for blessing, encouragement, healing, or any other thing. We may not understand what impressions You put on our hearts, yet we trust You and will pray anyway. Amen.

Praying What We Have Overcome

Once when my youngest son and I were waiting in line at the grocery store, the lady in front of us was struggling to keep her curious toddler from grabbing candy off the shelf while she attempted to put her groceries on the conveyor belt. When her determined young son managed to spill a whole box of gum, she tried to divert his attention to picking up after himself while she quickly finished her task, corralled him, picked up the last stray gum packets, and checked out. Seth looked at me and asked, "Did we ever put you through that?"

He heard stories all the way home. And then he apologized . . . though I can laugh when I think about those memories now.

When we remember challenges we've overcome, we have a double opportunity to pray. First, we thank God for bringing us through. We may not have even known He was at work, but He was—He always is! And He deserves our gratitude.

Second, knowing that others are now going through whatever we've successfully overcome, we can ask, from a heart full of the compassion uniquely born of experience, that God will help and encourage them. We may pray for someone we see, like the woman in the grocery store who was wrestling with her son. We may pray for someone we know of who is going through something we've faced. Or we may pray in general for anyone who happens to be going through whatever challenging experience we are remembering.

We all have troubles and struggles. When we remember those of our past, let's pause to pray.

Father, thank You for all You've brought us through in life so far. As we remember what You've done for us, remind us to pray for others who are facing the same circumstances now. Please help them as only You can. Amen.

Praying as We Pay the Bills

Whether we pay our bills monthly, bi-monthly, weekly, or as we go, we can use this activity as an opportunity to pray for ourselves and our communities. This is how:

First, *before* we write the checks or schedule on-line payments, we can take a moment to thank God for His provision. Everything we have comes from Him. We recognize this gratefully. Just as we pray before a meal to thank God for our food and ask His blessing on it, we can do the same as we prepare to spend our money. And while we are thanking Him for it and asking His blessing on it, we can recommit our money to Him and ask Him to help us use it wisely and responsibly. It is *His* money provided for our use as stewards (trusted servants) in His Kingdom.

Then, as we actually write the checks or schedule the payments, we can turn our prayers from gratitude, worship, and commitment to concern for others. We can pray for the companies we are sending money to. We can ask God to help them remember they exist to serve their communities, whether a small town, a big city, a state, the nation, or the *whole* world. We can ask God to bless their efforts and use them to fulfill His purposes for His kingdom even if they don't realize He is doing so. Let's thank God for enabling them to provide the goods or services they make available and ask Him to help them continue to do so, cost-effectively, with the good of the consumer, and therefore the entire community, in mind. Finally, we can and should ask God to raise leaders within these companies who will manage their businesses in a way that honors Him.

Second Chronicles 7:14 says, "If my people, who are called by my name, will humble themselves and pray and seek my face and turn from their wicked ways, then I will hear from heaven, and I will forgive their sin and will heal their land." When we pay our bills, let's take time to recognize God's Lordship over our finances and businesses and dedicate their use to Him that He can work among us and begin to heal our land.

Father, as we pay for what we need from businesses in our community, remind us to pray for that community and for those businesses. We are building Your kingdom where we live, after all. Please bless the people You have placed us among. Amen.

Praying over Our Family Schedule

Our families' schedules provide a significant opportunity for *Parachute Prayer*. This is true whether we're remembering their typical routine or praying about a particular event. Our families will benefit as we pray for each.

Therefore, as we go through our day, accomplishing our scheduled tasks, let's think about what different family members are doing at the same time and pray about those activities. Sometimes what they are doing will remind us of a need or of something we know God wants to see produced in their character or through their lives or of an opportunity they are trying to make the most of. Their tasks may also remind us to pray for their peers — teachers, co-workers, friends. As we think about what they are doing, prayer ideas will come to mind. Whisper them as you work — unless your task requires active use of your mind. It's easy to pray as you're washing the dishes, but not so much when you're balancing books.

If you don't know much about a family member's schedule, ask for information before that person leaves for the day. Ask in particular if there is any event for which that one would especially appreciate prayer. Sometimes, just knowing someone is praying can take some of the jitters away. God gave us our precious families. Let's support them with ongoing prayer.

Father, as we can, as we accomplish our given tasks, remind us to pray for loved ones who are working to complete theirs. Please provide whatever they need to succeed and to take a step closer toward becoming the people You've planned for them to be. Amen.

Praying for Familiar Ministries

My husband and I receive a lot of mail and e-mail from our church, our denomination, and an assortment of ministries we've been involved with or supported through the years. Sometimes, these ministries ask for money, but *more often* they offer resources, activities, and information. Like Paul, they are preaching the Gospel, spreading the Good News, offering people a better way of living, knowledge of Jesus, eternal, abundant life!

For me these have become a prompt for *Parachute Prayer*. Receiving such newsletters and flyers by whatever means they come reminds me to pray for these ministries. And sometimes, when I stop to pray for one, I pray for all—whichever ministries God's Spirit brings to mind at the time.

I invite you to join me! Let's pray for the churches and ministries that contact us. Let's pray that as they offer news and resources to others, God will provide all the resources they need to serve effectively. Let's pray for the health and well-being of each participant in the ministry and of their families. Let's pray that they'll conduct their business with wisdom and integrity—as God wants them to, as He leads. Most of all, as Paul requested, let's pray "that the message of the Lord may spread rapidly and be honored" (2 Thessalonians 3:1)—just as it was within each of us.

Consider these bonus words Paul also said:

"I urge you, brothers and sisters, by our Lord Jesus Christ and by the love of the Spirit, to join me in my struggle by praying to God for me." -Romans 15:30

According to this verse, we join the struggle and become participants in the ministries we pray for. It's a privilege to serve in this way!

Father, there are more ministries out there than we can choose to contribute to. Please show us where You'd like us to serve. Then remind us to pray for the others as we learn of their activities through mail, email, social media, or other means. May Your message spread rapidly and be honored all over the world. Amen.

Praying for Those Who Hurt

I have a workout DVD—I won't say it's new because I've had it for some time—but until recently, I'd been too intimidated to give it a try. The workout leader is one of my favorites and the DVD looked promising, but once I got it home, it looked scary, too.

I finally got up the courage to try the first workout, and I *loved* it! It was so much fun and not nearly as hard as the cover implied. The very next day, I tried the second routine.

Let's just say, I spent the rest of that day walking with a limp. Don't worry. I recovered quickly. Then I tried that routine again!

In the meantime, my little aches and pains reminded me that other people I know have little aches and pains, too. Some even have big aches and pains that won't go away as quickly as mine—if at all. I thought of them often as I recovered.

When we hurt, we must remember our God cares. Sometimes our God heals. Sometimes our God strengthens what is weak. And when He doesn't touch us physically, He's there to comfort, encourage, and strengthen from within. Always!

So when we hurt, let's pray for others—and believe that God will act. One way or another, He'll be there with the relief of His healing love.

Father, thank You for pain that reminds us to pray. And thank You for caring, for healing, for strengthening, for comforting, for encouraging, and for knowing just what each person needs. We trust You, Lord. Amen.

Praying When the Phone Rings

Today's prayer will be triggered by a familiar sound — your ringing phone. Times have changed, though. It used to be that all phones sounded the same. Then people started choosing their own cell phone ring tones. Now I have different ring tones for each family member. Unless it's someone outside the family, I know who's calling before I even find my phone.

If you've set your phone up the same way, whisper a prayer for the person who is calling as you reach to take the call. Otherwise, whenever the phone rings, whisper a quick, "Holy Spirit, please help me to say what You want me to as I take this call." Then think of the call, no matter who's calling, as a divine appointment — an opportunity to show someone God's love, encouragement, patience, and care. God's name may not be mentioned during the call, yet if we respond to the caller as God's Spirit wants us to, we become ministers-in-the-moment anyway. (This practice may be especially helpful both to us and to our caller if the call is from a telemarketer. May God bless us with grace to offer when we'd rather give a piece of our mind.)

As we develop this habit of calling on the Holy Spirit for help as we talk with people, we may also find ourselves breathing that prayer as we see people approaching us to talk in person or as we open letters and e-mails, too. After all, another person wanting to communicate with us is a privilege. It's also a prayer cue.

Father, help us to remember that phone calls are opportunities to share Your love, wisdom, patience, and strength. Whenever people call us, remind us to pray as we embrace the responsibility. Amen.

Praying When We Use Our Keys

I learned a new word while writing a blog post once. I wanted to write that I felt I'd been *lamblasted* during devotions that day, but then I got curious about the word. I looked it up. Turns out, the word is *lambasted*. And it doesn't mean quite what I thought it did at the time. The dictionary defines it as *sharply rebuked* or *reprimanded*. It can also mean *beaten severely* or *falling down drunk*.

None of these was what I was feeling about that morning's devotional experience *at all*.

Good thing I looked it up!

No. Devotions that day had a recurring theme. I did feel like I was hit with it again and again, but God wasn't rebuking or scolding. No. He was simply calling me to pray, a gentle reminder that I'd like to pass on to you.

Here are the verses I came across that day:

"I am not asking you to take them out of the world, but I ask you to protect them from the evil one. They do not belong to the world, just as I do not belong to the world. Sanctify them in the truth; your word is truth." –John 17:15-17, NRSV

"To set the mind on the flesh is death, but to set the mind on the Spirit is life and peace." –Romans 8:6

"Be alert and of sober mind. Your enemy the devil prowls around like a roaring lion looking for someone to devour." –1 Peter 5:8

Some of these are downright scary, don't you think? To set the mind on the flesh is *death*. The *devil prowls* around like a *lion* looking for someone to *devour*.

But we don't need to be scared. These verses warn us to protect our minds from the devil's lies, lies that can cause us spiritual and emotional harm. They also tell us that Jesus prayed for us and that God's Spirit is available to grant us life and peace. We only have to set our minds on Him. So let's pray!

We're praying for protection, so let's attach this *Parachute Prayer* to things that offer physical security. Whenever we put a key in a lock, enter an alarm code, or type in a password, let's whisper a prayer that God's Spirit will protect our minds and the minds of those we love. Let's ask for discernment— the ability to see clearly what is true. Following Jesus' example, let's ask that God will sanctify our loved ones in the Truth of His Word. Let's ask for His Spirit's influence and ever-growing control over the thoughts in invaluable minds. Finally, let's ask God to keep the devil *far away*. We were made for Jesus; our loved ones were, too. Our God has more than enough power to secure all who want to be safe.

Father, when we take action to protect ourselves physically or virtually, remind us to pray for Your protection of our and our loved ones' minds and emotions. There's some scary stuff out there. We need the security that only Your Spirit can provide. Amen.

Praying When Characters Remind You of Reality

Today's *Parachute Prayer* is one of my absolute favorites. It's the one that comes most naturally to me because I read a lot and this idea comes from that activity.

When we're reading a good book (or watching an interesting movie or TV show) and one of the characters reminds us of someone we know, we can pray for that person. It's as simple as that.

We can also pray if the character's circumstance reminds us of someone we know. Characters in books and movies are always finding themselves in pickles or facing crises that resemble, often in an exaggerated way, those that people deal with in real life.

And finally, if the character is struggling with painful emotions that remind us of a friend or family member who is coping with the same, we can pray for the person God brings to mind because of the book or show.

Naturally, God uses the Bible to bring lots of people to pray for to my mind. The story of Samson reminds me to pray for rebellious teenagers. Stories of David and Solomon remind me to pray for our nation's leaders. Psalms sometimes remind me of people dealing with harsh emotions. Paul's letters to Timothy remind me to pray for a few young ministry students I know.

But God doesn't limit Himself to the Bible for this purpose. Stories, both fiction and non-fiction, tell about life. And any given story may remind us of someone we know. When this happens, we can recognize it as a call to pray.

Father, we know that You bring people who need prayer to our minds through many means. Please let this be one of them! As we read, remind us of people for whom You'd like us to pray. And help us not be so engrossed in the words of the book or program that we pass up the privilege to pray. Remind us it only takes a moment to pause and whisper a caring prayer. Amen.

Praying over Precious Pictures

I love family photos. No — not going to get them taken. That can be a challenge to say the least. But I *love* having them around, all over my house, to remind me of the people I love the very most in our whole, great big, heavily populated world.

Because we live far from extended family, I especially appreciate pictures of the people I love dearly but don't get to see every day. I keep a special photo display devoted exclusively to these. Perhaps you have an arrangement like this in your home, too.

Today's *Parachute Prayer* is to let these favorite pictures remind us to pray for these priceless people. If you don't display photos all over your house like I do, then let a glimpse of the family photo album on the shelf or a digital slideshow on your computer bring close family members to mind. Whenever you think of them, remember to pray.

As a corollary to this concept, I'd like to share my grandmother's idea. If someone in your family is in need of specific or urgent prayer, keep that person's picture in your Bible for a time. Whenever you open your Bible, God can use the picture to call you to pray.

Father, You placed us in families. Remind us to pray for their members each day. Amen.

Praying for People without a Stable Home

The summer before my youngest son, Seth, left for college, he and my husband replaced the retaining wall along the side of our house. My son started the project by tearing the old wall down while my husband was at work. As Seth was doing this, he discovered a nest of chipmunks. The terrified creatures scattered everywhere!

For days after that, we saw the chipmunks frantically running around all over the yard, trying to find a new home. They finally settled in our wood pile. This was fine for a time.

Then the weather changed. We started enjoying fires in our fireplace, but the chipmunks became frantic again. Poor, little homeless things!

It occurred to me that some people have to live like that, too, moving from one temporary shelter to another, living in whatever somewhat comfortable space they can find until they're forced to move, longing for someplace to call home once again. Naturally, homeless people come to mind, but foster children often find themselves in this situation. Families struggling to make ends meet sometimes bounce from place to place, too.

When we see chipmunks or squirrels or stray cats roaming about our neighborhoods, let's thank God for the homes that we have and pray for those who are seeking a safe and stable place to live. Let's pray that God will lead them to a place where they can rest.

Father, thank You for our cozy homes. We're blessed to enjoy them. Let us not forget that not everyone has what we do. Please remind us to pray often for those who roam. Amen.

Praying When You Flip Light Switches

In the beginning, God said, "Let there be light," and there was and there is and there always will be. (See Genesis 1:3.) Our earth doesn't sit in physical darkness any more.

But there *are* dark hearts that don't yet know the Light of the World. That's why God sent Jesus.

Today's simple *Parachute Prayer* is that God will send His Light into the empty hearts all over this world. When you flip a light switch, turn on your headlights, open the blinds in the morning, or turn on your nightstand reading light at night, pray, "Lord, please let there be Light!" And I believe there will be someday.

True, each person has a choice, but let's pray that the Light will shine so brightly that people will be drawn to Jesus Christ and want all the Light He offers for *eternity*.

Father, if only we could simply flip light switches to brighten dark hearts. Thank You for sending Your Son for this task. Remind us to watch for opportunities to tell others about Your love and His sacrifice. Remind us even more often, through this simple symbolic act of turning on electric lights, to pray. Please let there be light! Amen.

Praying for Healthy Growth

"And Jesus grew in wisdom and stature, and in favor with God and man." –Luke 2:52

I've been praying Luke 2:52 for my children since they were born. I continue to pray it for them even now, though they've most likely reached their full stature by now. I want my children to grow like Jesus, and I know this is something God desires for them, too. Luke 2:52 covers every aspect of human growth:

In wisdom = mental growth
In stature = physical growth
In favor with God = spiritual growth
In favor with man = social growth

People who grow steadily in all four areas are well-rounded and healthy human beings indeed. So let's turn this verse into a *Parachute Prayer*!

First, if you haven't done so already, commit the verse to memory. You'll need to keep it in your brain for use whenever you're reminded to pray this prayer. It's an easy verse to memorize because it's short and it's a list. All you have to remember is that Jesus grew and that He grew in four ways: *in wisdom and stature, and in favor with God and man.*

Now here's the trigger. Whenever we see a ruler or a measuring device of any kind, let's let it remind us to pray. We can pray for our kids, for our grandkids, for our neighbors' kids, for kids who go to our churches, for nieces and nephews, and for our kids' friends.

We can also pray for grown-ups who are striving to grow in any of these areas. (When I do this, stature represents health in my prayer.) Until we reach Heaven, we all must strive to grow, prayerfully allowing God's Spirit to make us more like Christ. So from now on, whenever we see a measuring device, let's pause to pray.

Father, thank You for making people able to grow, and thank You for Jesus' example to follow. Please turn the measuring tools we use so often into reminders to pray about this process so crucial to all-around good health. Amen.

Praying about Angry Words

Not too long ago, my youngest son brought a blog post to my attention. It was written by a Christian entertainer who wanted to encourage Christians to do as Augustine and Wesley and others have encouraged: to be united in the essentials of our faith, but to show love in all else. This young artist simply wanted to see Christians love each other and get along in spite of different points of view.

Sadly, in offering examples of controversy among Christians, he made some vague statements that led some of his readers to question his personal beliefs. He didn't actually come right out and say what he, personally, believed or didn't believe about such things. But some of his readers, misunderstanding or misreading his intent, chose to fill in the blanks themselves. Next thing he knew, this artist who had simply asked for peace found himself under attack. It was a great big, ugly mess.

It broke my heart.

This artist wrote one response to defend himself which only brought more painful comments from readers. Since then (as I'm writing this), he has been quiet.

This breaks my heart, too. I fear he's facing the temptation to build a wall, to hide his gift, to protect himself when he has so much to share with the world. This would be a tragedy.

How amazing could the situation have turned out if those who questioned this young man's words would have taken the time, first, to try to see his heart, then, if necessary after gentle questioning, to prayerfully respond as Priscilla and Aquila did when Apollos didn't quite have all of his facts straight? (See Acts 18:24-28.)

Today's *Parachute Prayer* comes from this unfortunate situation. Knowing that behind every blog post, tweet, *Facebook* update, news headline, and book is a flesh and blood human being created in the image of God, let's pray for those who come under attack for the words they write — especially for those who come under such attack for simply trying to say something helpful, encouraging, or good. When we see negative comments or hear verbal criticism about something we've seen in print or published on the internet, let's pray both for the heart of the one receiving the criticism and of the one who delivers it. Let's pray that God will give wisdom to both, that He'll help the one who receives the negative words to hear anything necessary and to disregard the rest and that He'll guide anyone tempted to deliver a painful blow to take a step back to consider a more Christ-like response. If they've already delivered the painful blow, let's ask God to open their eyes to the wounds they've inflicted and lead them to set things right, if possible, and learn a better way for the next time.

People are imperfect, and their words can be messy, jumbled up, and completely misunderstood. Let's take the time to see the intent behind the words, to clarify what confuses, to show grace and compassion before jumping to judgment, and to correct (when it's called for) only as Christ would. And when we see angry words appearing in the comments about what we're reading on our computer screens, let's always remember to pray.

Father, please help readers to remember that there are people behind words they see and to respond to those people with love instead of to words indiscriminately. Thank You, Lord. Amen.

Praying before Tasks

Once when our family went bowling, my son asked why I stop, hold the ball up in front of me, and stare at the pins for a moment before *throwing* the ball. I told him I need to make sure everything is all lined up before I bowl. If I want the ball to hit that center pin, I have to keep it all lined up. (I don't accomplish this very often, but at least I start in the right place.)

In Genesis 24:12, we read how Abraham's servant stopped and lined things up, too. When Abraham sent him to find a wife for Isaac, the servant asked God for success — and he did this for Abraham's sake!

"Then he prayed, 'O Lord, God of my master Abraham, make me successful today, and show kindness to my master Abraham.'" –Genesis 24:12

We can do this, too. Before we begin any task, let's pause and pray — to line things up — for Jesus' sake!

Many of us already pray before we eat or before we go on a trip. Here are a few more ideas:

- Before we do our devotions, we can ask God to reveal what we need to see.
- Before we shop, we can ask God to help us find what we need and spend wisely.

- Before we write that message, we can ask God help us choose words that encourage others and honor Him.

- Before we send our family out the door, we can ask God to go with them, blessing their day.

Lord, remind us to pause and pray before we do anything, that everything we do will honor You. We are Your servants. Please grant us success (by Your definition) for Your sake. Amen.

Praying before Meals

Eating, while necessary to keep us alive, is also a metaphor for one of God's truths.

You see, every time we eat, something has to die. Whether it's a carrot or a cow, it gives its life, so we can live. (Milk would be the one exception, but the cow has to eat something that has to die in order to make the milk, so the rule still applies.)

If we attempted to live without food, we would fail. Our bodies would die. For us to live, *something* must sacrifice its life.

Likewise (here's the metaphor), if we attempt to live without Christ, our souls die.

He died, so we can live — kinda, sorta, just like our food died. But He rose again and lives within us, and we feed on His Word daily that we can live abundantly until His return when we will live eternally.

And we'll no longer need food.

Though all the talk of feasting in the Bible leads me to believe we'll get to enjoy it anyway!

In the meantime, whenever we offer grace at a meal, let's thank God not only for the food but also

for His Son, our Savior. When you eat, be thankful—
and remember Jesus, *always*.

*Father, we have so much to thank You for! When we
pause to thank You for our food, remind us to thank You
for all of Your gifts, especially for Jesus and the
relationship that sustains our soul. Amen.*

Praying Bedtime Prayers

"Now I lay me down to sleep . . ."

When I was little, I used to say this familiar prayer each night before bed. Then, as many children do, I'd add, "God bless Mommy and Daddy and my brother and Grandma and Grandpa and my other grandma and the hamster and the goldfish and the new kid who just moved in down the street. . ." and so forth and so on to cover everyone I could think of.

Sometimes we think children make such a long list to stall for time, trying to put off going to bed. But I think most who've grown up in Christian homes, knowing that God is watching over them, truly just want to be sure they've covered everyone. They want to entrust all those they love to God's never-failing care.

In other words, if our children are praying like this, we've taught them well. Eventually, they'll learn that God continues to watch over everyone whether they remember every name or not. They won't fear forgetting. They'll realize God is the all-powerful and responsible one, not them. They won't feel the need to mention every name, every night. They'll simply trust.

Yet even after adults have learned this lesson, it's good to revisit childhood from time to time. As we prepare to sleep, we can ask God to bless and care for all the loved ones He brings to mind. If we know of specific needs, we can linger to mention them. If all seems well, so far as we know, we can simply mention names, entrusting precious people to our ever-loving God.

I know. We're not supposed to choose a prayer time when we're likely to fall asleep. But bedtime doesn't have to be our *only* prayer time. This is a *Parachute Prayer,* practicing God's presence with a whisper anytime. I can think of no better way to fall asleep than in God's presence, letting Him close our eyes and tuck us in with thoughts Him and dearly loved people the last on our mind for the day.

"In peace I will lie down and sleep, for you alone, Lord, make me dwell in safety." –Psalm 4:8

Father, thank You for watching over all the people we love, every day, all the time. Bless their lives with an ever-

growing knowledge of You. Help us all to trust whether awake or sleeping in peace. Amen.

Praying Bedtime Prayers, Part 2

I often use my website, *Wildflower Faith*, to encourage readers to pray for the prodigals, to pray for the unsaved. Jesus is coming again someday. The Bible makes that clear. So we must pray diligently that God will draw many more people to join His Kingdom before that glorious day.

Yet Christians need to pray for each other, too. In 2 Thessalonians 1, Paul prayed that God would enable the Thessalonians, whose faith was flourishing and whose love for one another was growing (verse 3), to live lives worthy of His call. He asked that God would enable them to accomplish everything their faith prompted them to do (verse 11). Modern-day children of God need to pray that for each other, too.

Tonight as you're lying in bed, waiting to drift off into sleep, think of all the people you know who have *dreams* to accomplish for God. Then pray for those people. Ask God to help them live lives worthy of His call—if they don't, their ministry won't mean anything. Those who serve God must live lives of integrity. Ask God, also, to empower them to accomplish all the good things their faith prompts them to do—in God's time and according to His will.

As Paul prayed for the Thessalonians, let's pray for the people we know who have a vision for serving God.

Father, please help us to pray for each other faithfully just as Paul prayed for the Thessalonians. Help our Christian brothers and sisters to live the way You want them to. Give them dreams and faith promptings of serving You as only they can, as You designed them to. And please enable them by Your Spirit to do all that You call them to do. Amen.

Praying for Our People

I don't know if this is true of all dogs or not, but our dog has people.

What I mean is that there's a distinct difference in the way he greets *his* people and *other* people who come to our door.

When one of *his* people comes to the door, even if that person has been away for a long, long time — like on a deployment or because they've gotten married and settled on the far side of the universe — Windsor greets that person by bouncing all over the room, offering slobbery, dog kisses, and doing the ever-entertaining, elderly puppy dance of joy.

Once Windsor has identified someone as one of *his* people, Windsor never forgets.

If someone who is not one of Windsor's people comes to the door, though, he sniffs around suspiciously, ducks all attempts at friendly pats on the head, and sometimes even hides under the bed. (When he goes to this extreme, I have to wonder if maybe I should pay attention to his strange judgment call.)

Windsor's people include the obvious: immediate family, parents, brothers, sister, and, of course, our cross-country kids. And because the mail carrier lady brings so many for-review books to my door (which always puts a smile on my face), Windsor has adopted her as one of his people, too, greeting her joyfully and even attempting to follow her home. (I should probably learn her name.) I'm pretty sure that all small children are Windsor's people, too. If he sees them out the window, he wags his tail and begs to go play!

That said, I think it's safe to say we people have people, too — precious people whose lives will always be intertwined with ours in a deep and mysterious way. Today's *Parachute Prayer* is for them. Whenever your pet greets someone happily, whether your pet is a dog or a cat or a hamster or hermit crab, whisper a prayer for one of your precious people. (And if your cat, hamster, or hermit crab actually does greet someone enthusiastically without the bribe of a can of tuna or a *HoneyNut Cheerio*, I would sure love to hear about it because I'm pretty certain that only dogs admit to having people — but I may be wrong.)

If you don't have a pet, let glimpses of other people's pets prompt your *Parachute Prayer* or set a sweet, stuffed animal somewhere obvious to remind you. You have people! Keep thanksgiving for them in your heart and their names in your prayers always.

Father, whether we see our people daily or not, please remind us to pray for them often. We are gifts to each other from You! Bless each of the people You have placed in our lives. Thy will be done in theirs. Amen.

Praying for Prior Occupants

Unless you happen to live in a brand new home, someone else inhabited your current space before you did. (And, even if you're in a new home, someone, at some time, probably lived on your land, somehow.) As a result, you may come across evidence of your home's prior occupant from time to time.

For instance, my husband and I know that the man who lived in our home before we did, a man who died several years before his widow sold the house to us, enjoyed woodworking and considered himself to be something of a handy man. His family chose to leave behind a beautiful bookcase that he'd built. We love this hand-me-down!

He also had a tendency to *Mickey-Mouse* things that needed to be repaired. *Mickey-Mousing* is a useful skill — until the something you *Mickey-Moused* has to be repaired again and someone else has to figure out what you did, so they can undo it, then *Mickey-Mouse* a new repair of their own. *Mickey-Mousing* reminds us of our home's prior occupant.

(I wonder why we call it *Mickey-Mousing*. I'd really hate to think we're insulting the world's favorite mouse.)

Back to the *Parachute Prayer*: when you come across something that reminds you your current home had a previous occupant, pray for that person and his or her family. You may receive a piece of mail to return or find something left behind in the attic or on a high closet shelf. Maybe this person added a unique, yet permanent, personal touch. When you notice these, take a moment to pray.

You may not know the people who once lived in your home, but God does. He also knows their needs. A whispered prayer may make a difference in ways you'll never know.

Father, I know the man who built my bookshelves has gone on to eternity, yet his family lives on — and they were so proud of him. Help them to follow his example, leaving legacies of their own. And, if any among them don't know You, please open their eyes and their hearts to You. Thank You, Lord. Amen.

Praying while Driving

Praying for Our Neighborhood's Schools

I like to get started pretty early most mornings. If I have errands to run, I'm bound to go through several school zones, pass a few school busses, and even stop to wait while those busses pick up children beginning their day. If you are an afternoon person, you'll see and do the same as the routes run in reverse. Let's use these sights and actions as a call to prayer. When we see the bright yellow school zone signs or busses and begin to slow or stop, we can let them remind us to pray for the students, teachers, administrators, parents—even for government officials or groups that work together on our children's behalf.

The system might not be perfect, but it is impacting the next generation in a significant way. Therefore, we must pray—for the system and for those who function within it.

I know some of these people, the amazing members of our educational system. I'm even related to more than a few! They care about kids, want to make a difference in their lives, and are helping to set them on the path to a productive and fulfilling future. They deserve our prayers as they strive to do this.

Let's thank God for teachers like these — and ask Him to send more.

I also know some amazing kids — and just happen to be related to more than a few of those, too! In some cases, I can only imagine the challenges they face; so let's pray for the kids as well. They need all the strength and encouragement and wisdom they can get.

I've listed quite a bit to pray for during the 30 seconds or so it takes to drive through a school zone or wait for a bus, but that's the beauty of a *Parachute Prayer*. When we see signs of schools, we'll pray for whichever of these God brings to mind at the time. Together, with His help, we'll cover it all. When we see signs of schools, let's pray.

Father, please turn our waiting time and the impatience that sometimes goes with it into a meaningful few moments of prayer. Remind us that the people we are waiting for matter — adults and children alike. Please guide our thoughts, so we'll pray for what they most need. Amen.

Praying for Our Community's Churches

I notice a lot of churches when I drive down the road. Their signs make me think—sometimes laugh. For example:

Stop, drop, and roll doesn't work in hell.

If I hadn't been driving that would one have had me rolling on the floor, laughing out loud. It really tickled my funny bone. But then I remembered there really are those who, by their own choice, will suffer eternal separation from God—with no hope of relief. It was a sobering thought after all.

Trials are the food of faith.

Wow! That one comes straight from the book of James. What a profound paraphrase!

We'll never find a better friend than Jesus!

Yes! Thank You, Jesus, for being our best friend forever!

Today's idea is to pray for the churches we pass while driving down the road.

Whether we see steeples, crosses or quirky church signs, let's whisper a prayer on the church's behalf. It doesn't matter if the church is of our denomination or not. We're all in this together, growing in our knowledge of God and leading others His way.

And if we happen to catch the names of pastors on the signs as we drive past, let's offer specific prayers for them and for their families. God knows their needs; let's ask Him to provide.

We may also catch news of upcoming church events. Let's pray for their success — that the people the event is meant to reach will be drawn to come, that friendships will grow, that people will learn what God wants them to know, that He will make His presence known to all.

Father, church steeples, signs, and crosses are meant to remind us daily that You are in our midst. Please let these also call us to pray. Amen.

Praying for Misbehaving Drivers

Today's *Parachute Prayer* is going to be hard — at least for me.

I can't believe I thought of this. I'm maybe going to wish I hadn't.

But, I have to admit, it's probably a good idea — and I'm not taking the least, little bit of credit for it. (So please don't blame me when it becomes a challenge for you, too!)

Here goes:

A few moves ago, I've lost track of how many, I knew a lady who would pray for the drivers who misbehaved on the road. Seriously! When they turned in front of her or cut her off or refused to let her pass, she'd pray. Really! — she prayed *for* these people.

"Lord, that man's in a hurry. Please keep him safe. Please bless his day. Please bless his family. Please help him handle whatever is happening in his life today."

I always raised my eyebrow at her and secretly thought she was too good to be true — I suppose the eyebrow may have given me away.

But another friend recently mentioned having grace for other drivers on the road. If I remember correctly, she was confessing she didn't have much of that. I confess, sometimes I don't either.

But what better place is there to practice God's mercy and grace than out on the highway? The Bible says that as we judge, we'll be judged. For every complaint we may have made against another driver, others have probably made *some* complaint against each of us. We try to drive courteously and follow the rules, I know we do! But everybody makes mistakes. I appreciate grace when I do, therefore I should offer it when someone else does.

Did I just say that?

Grace for other drivers?

I'll give it a try if you will. Starting today, let's pray for other drivers — especially for those who should have their licenses revoked.

And let's not forget to drive courteously and carefully as we offer forgiveness and ask God to send blessings their way. Who knows? That other driver may be praying for us, too.

Father, as we carefully make our way to each destination, please remind us to offer grace and prayer for those around us, especially when they make mistakes that frighten us or slow us down. We're travelling together. Help us to prayerfully cooperate. Amen.

Praying for Yellow Ribbons

When my husband *was* deployed for the first time, I wanted people to pray for him. I also wanted people to pray for his unit and for all the soldiers stationed over there and for all the soldiers stationed anywhere else in this great big, often dangerous world. I still want people to pray. I know our soldiers need our prayers.

One day, as I pulled up to a stop light, I noticed one of those magnetic yellow ribbons on the back of the car in front of me. Usually they say, "Support Our Soldiers" or something along those lines, but this one said, "Pray for Our Soldiers." So I did. Then I went hunting for a magnetic yellow *Pray for Our Soldiers* ribbon of my own.* It wasn't easy to find, but I was determined. I figured if it prompted me to pray, it might do the same for someone else.

But if we're aware, the ribbon we see doesn't have to say, "Pray for Our Soldiers," to remind us to pray. When we see a yellow ribbon magnetically attached to a car or a fabric one tied around a mailbox or tree, let's take a moment to pray. It's good to know our soldiers are always in God's care.

Father, the yellow ribbons are there to welcome soldiers home and to remind people that some are not. When we see yellow ribbons anywhere, please use them also to remind us to pray. Amen.

*I need to add a small public service announcement here for my fellow Army spouses whose soldiers are stationed overseas. Please notice that my ribbon didn't say, "Please pray for my soldier in Iraq" or anything else that indicated he was away. As we pray for the safety of our soldiers, let's make safe choices of our own and practice *family force protection* at home. Announcing to the world that your spouse is gone, no matter how proud you are, can be a dangerous thing.

Praying When We Drive Past What We Wish Weren't There

I'm pretty certain that most every town has, along with its nice establishments, well, its not-so-nice establishments — businesses that many of us wish would just go away, those we'd label as immoral, corrupt, rough, or sketchy. I've even seen some of these from the highway in the middle of nowhere while on road trips. They often post huge billboards advertising what they have to offer in their seedy, run-down shacks.

These, friends, are a call to pray.

When we must drive by these businesses or billboards, let's pray first for the spiritual health of our communities. More people living faithfully for Jesus means fewer customers for these businesses which means less opportunity for them to do people harm.

Next let's pray that God will give people tempted to patronize those businesses the strength and desire to resist that temptation. We can also pray for those who have already yielded, asking God to reveal the damage they are doing to themselves and to others.

Let's pray that God will bring them to their senses, helping them see why such is wrong.

Finally let's pray for the victims of behavior encouraged by these businesses: family, friends, innocents who get dragged into the mess and experience physical and emotional pain. I could expound upon that and go off on a rant, but I don't think I need to. I'm simply asking you to pray.

Father, it hurts to see evidence of sin in our towns — especially the evidence that others are being enticed into what can only cause pain. When we drive past these businesses, please remind us to pray, always. Amen.

Praying through Construction Zones

It seems wherever we are, we have a construction zone between our home and post. This means we have to drive through it — a lot. Which means slowing down — a lot. Heavy sigh.

Our lives are construction zones, too. God is hard at work turning willing Christians into the people He wants them to be. Sometimes He has to slow them down to do so. Sometimes He tears something down to build something else up — and sometimes this hurts.

So as we slow down to drive through road construction zones (or drive past building construction sites), let's pray about the work that God is doing in people's lives. God may bring specific people to mind or even groups of people. If so, pray for them. If not, pray generally that people will patiently allow God to work as He constructs amazing things.

Father, thank You for working faithfully, all around us, all the time. Continue to build on Christ in our lives. Thy Will be done . . . and Lord, please keep the road crews and people driving through their construction zones safe.

Those can be dangerous places. Please watch over people and protect them, too. Amen.

Praying for Movers

On a cross-country road trip a few years ago, I was surprised to note how many people actually move Beverly Hillbilly style. On occasion we've done this, too, as we tend to underestimate the space our stuff will need. It was comforting to know we're not the only ones who tie stuff to the roof or leave it hanging out the windows and back of the truck in a desperate attempt to take it all with us!

On this same trip, we also got to watch our oldest son leave the world of college, driving off with his first little U-Haul for his very first apartment on his own, all by himself, in the real world. The U-Haul was *so cute!* Watching our eldest drive off with it reminded me of seeing him wearing his first little pair of shoes! So much potential! The shoes grew. The U-Haul will, too. Our son is embarking on yet another new phase of his life. *Thank You, Lord! Please go with him wherever he goes as he lives to honor You always. Amen.*

As I was driving onto the freeway yesterday, I noticed a car pulling a U-Haul the size of my son's and wondered if the driver was another first-apartment-bound college graduate or what other purpose that moving trailer served. I said a little prayer for the person in the car. Then, as I traveled down the road, I noticed other moving trailers and trucks, each representing someone's transition from one place to another. This led me to today's *Parachute Prayer*:

When we see moving trailers and trucks, let's breathe quick prayers for relocating families. Whatever their circumstances, happy or sad, simple or complex, transition is a challenge. Let's ask God to help these movers handle it well.

Father, our lives are full of change. Please be with those who are moving today. Protect their families and their belongings, lead them into a good land, and help them happily find their place. And Lord, if they don't know You, please use this event to make Yourself known, to draw them to You. Prepare their hearts for the ultimate move — into Your presence in eternity someday. Thank You, Lord. Amen.

Praying When We See Gas Station Signs

Whenever I drive into town, I'm greeted by our local gas station's ultra-large, neon green sign declaring the latest, usually-bad news about the price of gas. Talk about a call to pray!

When we notice changing gas prices, for good or for ill, let's let them remind us to pray. Let's pray, not only about rising expenses, but also for the recovery of our economy, for people who are struggling to make ends meet or desperately seeking jobs, and that God will continue to meet the needs of His people when times are hard.

Father, that neon sign reminds me that many people are finding it more and more difficult to afford the things they need. Please provide – fuel for necessary transportation, food, clothing, homes, jobs, and healthcare – all of our basic necessities. And please help those in power, those with the ability to make a difference, to make wise decisions in order to move things (like gas prices and such) in a more positive direction to benefit all. We thank You, Lord, for Your provision, love, and care. Amen.

Praying for Victims of Abuse

While out running errands one day, I noticed a car stopped across the intersection that had some truly unusual dents. It didn't look like it had been hit by a car. The paint wasn't damaged. But both driver's-side doors had people-sized indentations–like two people had literally thrown themselves up against the car with all the force they had. I can't imagine anything else that would have made dents like that. Knowing that people don't throw themselves up against cars just for fun, I'm pretty certain that the situation which resulted in the damage to that car also resulted in some damage to people. It probably wasn't a pleasant sight, and people may still be recovering both physically and emotionally.

These thoughts prompted a new *Parachute Prayer*. When we see dents in cars, let's pray for damaged people–people who suffer from physical, verbal, and/or emotional abuse. Except in the case of extreme physical abuse, we may never see the wounds these people have received. The bruises are real, however, and these people are hurting.

If you have time, add prayers for those who self-inflict such pain. Pray that people who care will notice and gently steer them toward the help they need–or that they'll recognize the need for such help themselves.

Finally, don't forget to pray for those who abuse. Those who hurt others usually do so because they are hurting or because they have been hurt. Pray they'll recognize their own suffering in the eyes of those they abuse. Pray they'll choose to stop hurting others and seek healing. Pray they'll seek forgiveness, too, from God and from those they've wounded.

Father, this world is full of pain and sometimes people are cruel. Please bring an end to such suffering! Protect those who are being abused. Lead them to shelter. Help them to recognize their value in Your eyes and to seek refuge in You and with people who can help them escape. Stand up for those who are helpless by helping others to see what they are suffering. Bring hidden pain to light that victims can be saved. And please cause those who inflict pain to realize that what they are doing is wrong. Prompt them to do what they must to stop. We thank You for seeing what we don't. We thank You for caring always! We pray that You'll act to bring relief in all situations. Thank You, Lord. Amen.

Praying When Caught in Traffic

Once when we were caught in traffic, my husband asked me if I had any *Parachute Prayers* for the situation. I told him about a few of the praying-while-driving prayers. Later I realized that when I'm driving through heavy traffic, I automatically pray. This is especially true if traffic is suddenly required to merge from five lanes to two because of road construction or to navigate around an accident. This situation can be tense. It's not unusual for minor accidents to result. And so, I pray.

Whenever we find ourselves carefully maneuvering our vehicles through traffic jams, let's first ask God to keep us calm and aware. Let's ask Him for His protection and help. Then let's pray the same for all the drivers around us. It's when people become impatient that fender benders occur, and these only make a frustrating situation worse. So let's ask God for plenty of patience and wisdom. Let's ask Him also to give everyone plenty of grace toward each other. Let's ask Him to help us be courteous — even when others are not. Let's keep up the praying until we break free.

I've found the greatest benefit to this *Parachute Prayer* is the sense of calm and camaraderie that it gives me. I'm in the situation with many others, and we all want out. I ask God to help us work together, so we can all safely reach our goal. Then I do my part by driving carefully.

Father, when we must maneuver through tough traffic situations, remind us to ask for Your help. The Fruit of the Spirit (Galatians 5:22-23), especially peace, patience, kindness, gentleness, and self-control, is a useful gift for all as we work together to get where we need to go. Amen.

Praying when Out and About

Praying as Things Change

Always with Autumn comes an abundance of seasonal shopping displays: back to school, Halloween, Thanksgiving, Christmas . . . One of our local stores got so carried away with this last year that they actually started putting out Valentines before the New Year. I guess they just couldn't wait to start promoting the next big thing.

Personally, I love the Autumn displays. Except for when I've lived in climates where I knew Autumn leaves meant I was about to be buried in snow for months on end, I've always appreciated all signs of the end of Summer — including store displays.

When we notice these, let's let them remind us to pray. Changing displays signal other changes, too: changes in season, changes in activities, changes in temperature, changes in clothing styles, changes in décor. So let's pray for people we know who are going through some kind of life change. This list could include people who are moving or going to college for the first time, people who are changing jobs or struggling through divorce, and people who are adapting to changes brought on by illness or injury.

As we recognize changes in familiar store displays, let's remember that lives all around us are ever-changing, too. Let's ask God to help the people we love find peace with what is new.

Father, change is inevitable. Some changes are welcome, but others bring pain. When we notice the subtle changes all around us, please remind us to pray for those who are struggling. Thank You, Lord, for caring. Please make us aware, so we'll learn to be caring, too. Amen.

Praying over Our Family Trees

For my middle son's 9th birthday, our extended family gathered to celebrate at a neighborhood park. At one point during the afternoon, Alex decided to climb way up into a high tree. Then he called down and waved at the grown-ups below. My grandmother clutched her chest and said, "Oh, my Lord! Please help him."

There was a collective gasp from all of her children, grandchildren, and great-grandchildren who heard. Grandma was confused at the horrified looks she was getting until someone whispered to her that she'd taken God's name in vain.

Grandma became quite indignant and defended herself. "I was praying to my Lord. Alex could have broken his neck."

We all decided to take Grandma's word for it. It would have been very out of character for her to take God's name in vain. (Hence the community gasp.)

Alex climbed down safely, by the way. But ever since that day, climbing trees have reminded me to pray.

When we see climbing trees in parks or along the roadway, let's pray over our family trees. I don't know if you've noticed, but families tend to have both what-seem-to-be-hereditary talents and sins. They aren't really hereditary, but behaviors, decisions, personality traits, means of handling stress or conflict, personal interests, and such are often passed down from one generation to the next to the next. These won't be evident in all family members, of course, but they will be seen in a majority.

Can you identify some of these in your family? If they're positive, offer thanks to God whenever you see a climbing tree. Ask Him to help this strength continue within your family.

If you're seeing something negative, you can pray against this. Ask God to break your family free of this for good, starting with your generation. Pray often. Pray with determination. God's Spirit helped you to recognize this problem; He wants to help You pray to purge it out of Your family.

Father, we thank You for our families, for each branch of the family tree. Please show us what seems to be hereditary and help us to pray for its continuation or removal, according to Your ways. We love You, Lord. We thank You for loving our families. Amen.

Praying for Tabloid Victims

Today's *Parachute Prayer* may seem a little silly in light of world crises like hunger, homelessness, and tragic events. Yet when you consider the influence the following group of people tends to have on our children and teens—often impacting the way they dress, talk, behave, and believe—praying for these people may help make a difference, not only in their lives, but also in the lives of our kids.

So when we're in the check-out line at the grocery store and find ourselves assaulted by celebrity gossip in magazine headlines, instead of reading the headlines (which are probably exaggerated or mostly untrue), let's pray for the *people* whose pictures we see. God created and cares about celebrities, too, whether they're behaving or not, in the limelight by choice or circumstance. For some celebrities, having gained the whole world, perhaps prayer—that leads to God—is all they need.

Father, please give us compassion for these people who seem so privileged. They have needs, too. In fact, they may need more than we do. And if they don't, they need Your guidance in using what they've been given for the glory of

Your name. Help us to remember that all people need prayer, even these. When we recognize their pictures, please lead us to pray. Amen.

Praying for Those Who are Lost

As I was leaving Wal-Mart one day, I noticed their missing children's board. A sign near the bottom proudly proclaimed, "8,062 recovered."

"Thank You, Lord," I prayed, "and please help those who seek them to find all the rest!"

At that moment, my mind made a dramatic connection between the physically missing and the spiritually missing. Jesus, our Good Shepherd, is seeking lost sheep. (See Luke 15:3-7.) These are the people God created, each to be His child yet living outside His Kingdom. He leaves the 99 to find the one, but the 99 need to pray, for they are safely in God's hands, while the one is in grave danger — literally. (Yes — there are so many more than one, yet the parable shows how important each individual is to Christ. If only for one, He still would have died. He loves *each* person that much.)

So, just as Wal-Mart is keeping the faces of missing children before the public in order to recover as many as possible, let's keep the faces of spiritually lost loved ones and friends before our Heavenly Father through prayer. Put out an Amber Alert! Keep a list in your journal and prayerfully review it regularly. Then, whenever you pass Wal-Mart's missing children's board or see an Amber Alert on your phone or TV, pray for the children, then pray for lost sheep. The danger to both is urgent and real, the consequences eternal in the case of sheep not found.

Father, remind us to pray daily for the unsaved of this world, that we can rejoice with the angels in heaven as that recovered number climbs. Amen.

Praying While Waiting

As much as I love reading, reading in a waiting room to pass the time is something I can rarely do. (That doesn't stop me from taking a book along—just in case.) In a small room full of strangers, waiting for my name or one of my children's names to be called, I'm much too easily distracted to focus on a book, no matter how fascinating its storyline may be. Instead, I'm learning to use the time to pray for the people around me. The following account is an example of how this works out:

Once when my son and I reported for his annual eye exam, we found ourselves waiting in a small room, fairly crowded for its size. A young woman walked into the waiting room and sat down next to me. She began talking to everyone in the room, to anyone in general who happened to be listening, about why she was there. No. She'd never worn glasses before, but she couldn't read the sign on the wall across the room from where we sat, so she was sure she needed them. She was glad she was there.

I found it curious that this young woman was broadcasting this information to everyone in the room, but I figured she must be nervous. Poor thing! I silently breathed a prayer that God would calm her nerves and strengthen her eyes.

She was still talking. Now she was telling everyone that she was newly married, just a few weeks! I prayed about that, too, asking God to bless her marriage and make it last. He'd joined two people together; I asked Him to grow the marriage healthy, loving, and God-honoring.

About that time the optometrist came out and invited an elderly woman to go in for her exam. "Why Mrs. [fill in the blank], it's good to see you again. Hasn't been very long. What can I do for you today?" The door closed behind them. I figured she'd been there a lot, since the doctor seemed to know her so well, so I asked God to help the doctor help her eyes, however they needed helping.

Are you starting to get the idea? It's not that I'm intentionally being nosy, but if I find myself waiting in a room full of people, why not use the information that is presented and offer prayers on the people's behalf?

So when we find ourselves waiting in confined spaces, for the dentist, for the bus, in a check-out line, even at a red light, let's make it our practice to whisper prayers for the people around us. We don't have to know them or anything about them because God knows *everything*. Let's ask Him to give them whatever it is they need and to bless them with His presence as they go on their way.

Father, we're surrounded by people in so many of the places we go. Grant us the gift of observation and lead us to quietly pray for people who are also waiting in the space where we are. Amen.

Praying When Unseen or Ignored

Today's *Parachute Prayer* was passed on to me through my oldest son. When he was a student, Justin led a ministry to the homeless in his city through the university he attended. He befriended some of the people on the streets and enjoyed visiting and talking with them. One man told him that he likes to cheerfully smile and say, "Hi," to people who walk by, but that people often ignore him, look down, or even look away. He said this used to hurt his feelings, but he came to see it as a call to pray. He prays that God will bless these people, whatever they are doing, wherever they are going, whatever they need. He places busy people in God's hands.

Did you catch that? This homeless man prays for *everyone else* — especially for those who pretend he isn't there. I think that's pretty cool. God has blessed that man with grace.

Homeless people aren't the only ones who get slighted from time to time. We all encounter people, sometimes, who are busy, grumpy, or simply preoccupied. Instead of dwelling on hurt or anger when people ignore us or avoid our attempts at cheerfulness, let's follow this man's example and accept the invitation to pray.

Then let's follow that up with an extra prayer or two for the homeless, the abused, the neglected, and the destitute. Let's ask God to provide for their needs — then help out however we can.

Father, help us turn our hurt feelings into a gracious prayer offering whenever we feel ignored. Amen.

Praying When People Sneeze

Whenever someone in my household sneezes, no matter what room they're in or how far away from me, I make it a point to say (or yell), "Bless you!" I take this very seriously — in a quirky kind of way.

So, if I sneeze, and no one blesses me, I either bless myself (in a passive-aggressive, yet happy way — Passive-aggressive because they didn't bless me, but happy because the sneeze made me think of Jesus) or I yell, "Hey! No one blessed me!" Someone usually does.

Now I know the custom of saying, "Bless you," is based in pagan superstition, something about the sneeze making you vulnerable to evil things. But that's not why I say, "Bless you." If Jesus is in our hearts, sneezes and evil things have no power over us at all. As I said in the last paragraph, sneezes make me think of Jesus — thanks to this odd custom. And I think God kinda, sorta likes it a whole lot whenever we bless each other in His Name. We should do this every chance we get!

So when we hear a sneeze, let's use the opportunity. Let's ask God's blessing on whoever is nearby.

Father, thank You for reminding us to pray for good things for each other — through whatever means necessary — even through a common sneeze. Amen.

Praying for Your Church

Every four years, representatives from around the world gather to make decisions on behalf of all the churches in our denomination. Their primary purpose is to glorify God. They also strive to keep unity in the Church by educating and inspiring. Groups of people with common ministries and interests meet together in smaller groups. Choosing new general superintendents to replace any who are retiring is something that catches the interest of all.

It occurs to me that this is something to pray about.

On a smaller scale, districts within our denomination assemble once a year. Local boards meet at least once a month.

Obviously, I don't know what church you attend, but I do know that all churches must have meetings like this of some kind. Whenever they do, we must pray. When they must choose new leaders, whether superintendents, pastors, associates, deacons, board members, or small group facilitators, we must pray. When those leaders have decisions to make on behalf of the church, we must pray. God has a vision for each church. Let's ask Him to help our leaders see it as big and small decisions are made.

Father, thank You for our churches, for the opportunity to choose its leaders and participate in the decision-making process whenever this needs to be done. Regardless of our particular roles, remind us, first and foremost to pray. You are the Sovereign Ruler over all. Amen.

Praying while Waiting for Worship to Begin

As I was sitting quietly, waiting for worship time to start one day, I noticed a young woman sitting a few rows ahead of me and remembered that we'd prayed for her recently. Knowing that her situation hadn't yet changed, I whispered another prayer for her. When I finished, I noticed another friend with another known need and whispered another prayer.

As I continued to wait for the service to start, God's Spirit seemed to direct my attention around the room to remind me of others who had recently requested prayer. I was blessed to find myself in a quiet place where I could remember these needs and share them with God once again. Later, reflecting on the experience, it occurred to me God had shown me another *Parachute Prayer*.

When we're quietly waiting for an event to start, when we've moved past the time to be social and into the time of anticipation, let's ask God to remind us of the needs of those who are sitting nearby. Then let's offer silent prayers on their behalf. Let's anticipate not only the service, program, or event, but also God's answer to the prayers of people we know.

Father, thank You for the privilege of intercessory prayer — that we can tell You about the needs of people around us, that You know those needs and hear our prayers, that You always care and always act bringing about Your very best in Your perfect time. When we see people with needs of which we're aware, please remind us to pray right then. Amen.

Praying for Young Servants

Often in church, I'll notice that several teens from our congregation serve as volunteers. They greet people and hand out bulletins, sing and play guitar with the praise team, set up and help with sound, take up the offering, and play the piano offertory. I also know of many who help behind the scenes. Their service is crucial not only for the church but also for their spiritual well-being — they are learning that they have a place of service in the church *now* while also developing habits of volunteering for a *lifetime* of ministry in God's Kingdom.

Hopefully, these youth realize they are valued by God the Creator who gave each one gifts to use. He loves them simply for who they are: His unique creation. But He loves it when they offer, as soon as they are able, to serve Him as they can. I love seeing them do this on Sunday, scrambling all over the church.

And so, today's *Parachute Prayer* regards these young people. When we notice them using their talents for God, let's remember to pray for them. They are walking on the right path with so much potentially ahead. Let's pray that God will bless their efforts and reward them fully with the satisfaction and peace that comes from doing a job well. Let's pray that they will know they are loved and valued both by God *and* by His church. Then let's take time to thank them for being faithful servants He can use — servants, brothers, and sisters in the Kingdom of our Lord.

Father, thank You for teenagers, children, and young adults who are already finding ways to use their gifts for You. Bless their efforts. Increase their abilities. Help them to work well with others in Your Kingdom, regardless of age. Most of all, please let them know they are living in Your presence – the God Who Sees. Thank You for loving them, Lord. Help them to experience this love for themselves as they faithfully share it with others. Continue to lead them in all Your ways. Amen.

Praying for Look-Alikes

I was taking our dog to the groomer. When I walked into the office, I was startled to see a good friend of the family's slightly-older-than-teenage daughter sitting at the receptionist's desk. (I was startled because I haven't seen this girl in a few years, and she lives on the other side of the United States!) But it wasn't really her, after all. They say everyone has a look-alike somewhere in this world. That day I met our friends' daughter's.

And God seemed to say, *"Pray for her!"*

So I did. I prayed for our friends' daughter, then I prayed for her look-alike (all while trying to hand off an overly excited, wiggly puppy dog). I didn't know anything about the look-alike, but I asked God to make her as much like the girl I did know on the inside as on the outside because the girl I know is loving Christ and serving Him with all her heart each day.

When we see someone who reminds us of someone else, that's a cue for a *Parachute Prayer*.

And while we're praying for look-alikes, just for fun, why not pray for our own?! After all, they do say we all have one. (I don't know who *they* are, but if *they* say it's true, it *could* be so, don't you think? — Okay, normally I'd tell you to check it out when *they* say it's true, to make sure it really is, but this is just for fun — no harm, no foul.)

Father, please bless our look-alikes today — wherever they happen to be! If they don't know you, please draw them into Your kingdom. And if they do, please bless them with an extra-close sense of Your loving presence. Thank You, Lord! Amen.

Praying by Bead

A few years ago, I received a unique Christmas gift from a friend. It was a bracelet made up of beads of all different colors, shapes, and sizes. I still enjoy it. It's very pretty, but it serves a purpose, too.

My friend explained that it's kind of a Protestant adaptation of Catholic rosary beads, meant to help us pray more faithfully. The first bead is small and black. That one reminds me to confess and repent of any sin in my life and to pray for people who haven't yet turned away from sin. All of the other beads are up for grabs! In other words, if I have a prayer concern, I assign it to a bead. Whenever I see that bead, I remember to pray. The beads can represent specific people *or* needs, whatever or whomever I'm praying for on a given day.

I love this! If I'm standing in line or sitting at a red light or watching a boring movie on TV, I can fiddle with my beads — and pray!

But you don't need a beaded bracelet to put this idea into practice. Here's another way:

When you have a specific prayer concern, assign a color to it. (You may want to make a list for yourself to keep track.) Then when you're standing in line or sitting at a red light or watching a boring movie on TV, notice the colors around you — and pray!

Or:

Put a household object representing your prayer concern in an unusual place to remind you to pray. For example, if your child is facing a daunting test at school, put a textbook, dictionary, or graded paper in your refrigerator or beside your bathroom sink. Whenever you see it, pray!

How often do we tell people we'll pray for them or intend to pray more fervently about something and then simply forget? We get busy and are easily distracted. These simple reminders can help us with that.

Father, we want to keep our word when we tell others we'll pray. We also want to remember important prayers we mean to regularly pray. Help us to find reminders, whether beads or colors or strangely placed things. Please find us faithful always. Amen.

Praying for Unborn Children

A funny thing happens in military circles about nine months after any deployment ends: babies seem to show up all over the place! I just love these baby seasons. New, sweet, little people to meet and watch grow just bouncing all over the place.

It never fails, whenever I see a woman who's expecting a baby, I'm reminded of others I know. This has led to one of my favorite *Parachute Prayers*.

Whenever we see an expectant mother, we can pray for her and for her unborn child. Then we can pray for other expectant mothers we know, adding prayers for their children, both those born and unborn. We can pray for safe deliveries, healthy upbringings, early knowledge of Christ, and so much more. Jesus said, "Let the little children come to me." (See Mark 10:14.) Let's make it a practice to take them and their mothers to Him in prayer.

Father, thank You for babies and for the mothers You use to bring them into this world. When we see that a baby is on the way, please lead us to pray. Amen.

Praying for Our Grown Children

My youngest son drives a ~~cute~~ sporty, little silver car. (I know the make and model, but couldn't pick it out of a lineup. This is significant to this *Parachute Prayer*.) My middle son drives a moped and saves a ton of money on gas. My oldest son drives an airplane! (Okay, he *flies* an airplane and *drives* a red truck. But I couldn't pick his truck out of a lineup either, and airplanes are much easier to spot.) My daughter-in-law drives a ~~sporty~~ ~~cute~~ no, better-go-with-sporty-or-risk-offending-her-husband, gray car.

Let's bookmark that information. I'll get back to it. I need to tell you about my son who drives the airplane first.

Justin and his wife, Bridget, live clear on the other side of the United States from where my husband and I are. For whatever reason, our incomprehensible, but trustworthy God has placed us, for the time being, just about as far away from each other while all remaining in the United States as we can possibly be.

A moment of silence please. Now maybe a sad violin or two. I think I may need a tissue. Sniff.

Happily for me, God has provided an encouraging gift for such a time as this. A small airport lives just a few blocks away from me, even though Justin and Bridget don't. I often see planes like Justin's flying in or out, and when I do, I smile, think of Justin and Bridget, then offer a prayer or two.

And, as my nest is emptying out, I'm allowing mopeds to remind me to pray for Alex and sporty, little silver cars to remind me to pray for Seth. (You see? If I had to take the time to figure out what kind of sporty, little silver car I was seeing, I might forget to pray. Besides that, if I include *all* silver cars, I have even *more* reminders to pray! There's sound logic to being less specific here.) Red trucks and gray cars remind me to pray for Justin and Bridget, too.

If you have grown children, let vehicles like theirs remind you to pray for them. If this doesn't apply to you, just think of other people you care about and the vehicles they drive. Pray for spouses, parents, or close friends with specific needs. Let's let seeing familiar vehicles start reminding us to pray.

Father, thank You for our kids and for reminding us to pray for them. Bring them to mind often throughout each day. Amen.

Praying for Our Hearts

"I will give you a new heart and put a new spirit in you; I will remove from you your heart of stone and give you a heart of flesh." -Ezekiel 36:26

Though most *Parachute Prayers* are meant to remind us to pray for other people, sometimes we need to pray for ourselves. And if we're trying to follow Jesus who told us to love God above all others and to love our neighbors as we love ourselves (Mark 12:29-31), I think praying about the condition of our hearts is one of the most important prayers we can pray for ourselves. This world is designed to harden our hearts, to turn them to stone, to keep us from loving anyone well. This is something we must guard against (Proverbs 4:23).

Keeping this in mind, when we see stones, whether pebbles in a stream, rocks used as decorations outside a store or home, or boulders built into monuments, let's pause and ask God to soften our hearts. Then, when time allows, let's use that time to examine our hearts more thoroughly, giving God the time He needs to fully answer that prayer. Heart surgery can't be done in a moment, but the *Parachute*

Prayer can initiate the process, so God's Spirit can begin to work, letting us know what attitudes need to change, so He can soften our hearts.

Father, thank You for designing us with a great capacity to love. Help us to protect our hearts, so we can continue to love You and others well. Please reveal any hardness in our hearts. Then show us how to cooperate with Your Spirit, so You can bring healing. Teach us to love as You do. Amen.

Appreciating the Master

The next time you see a work of art — a painting, a sculpture, or some such masterpiece — pause to consider the work the artist put into it. Each brushstroke, each cut into stone, each smooth curve — the artist puts serious thought into every detail of a creation.

When I pause to reflect on the artist at work, my thoughts naturally turn to my Creator and His work and all we take for granted. He plans. He designs. He configures. He molds. Sunsets. Flowers. Creatures that fly and crawl and run and climb. People — each one as unique as the legendary snowflake.

Today's *Parachute Prayer* is to let the works of art you see draw you from appreciation of the piece to thoughts about its creator to worship of Your Creator, the greatest artist of all.

Father, Your works are wonderful. We know that full well (Psalm 139:14). *Thank You for giving us all things to enjoy* (1 Timothy 6:17) *and for using this enjoyment to draw us closer to You. We love You, Lord! Amen.*

Praying for Urgent Needs

Praying for Emergencies

Today's idea is one that's been on my mind since I started offering these suggestions on my first blog. I hesitated to write about it because it seemed so obvious to me. Then I realized it's obvious to me because it was the first prayer idea of this kind ever suggested to me.

I was in seventh grade. My Sunday school teacher, a beautiful, young newlywed that every girl in the class wanted to grow up to be *just like* decided to skip the lesson in order to spend the time mentoring her small group of junior high girls. She started by sharing some important tidbits of information, such as, "A young woman should never scratch under her armpits or dig wax out of her ears in public." (I'm not sure why she felt compelled to teach us this, but I was sitting in the front row of the class. Perhaps there was something going on behind me that I couldn't see.)

Next she began to teach us about prayer. She told us we could and should pray all the time about any and every little thing. She told us God is all around us to listen and hear and respond at any moment.

As she was explaining this, our lesson was interrupted by the sound of a siren going by. Our classroom window was open, so we had to wait for the emergency vehicle to pass. As the noise faded into the distance, our teacher told us that siren was our cue to pray. Someone was in trouble — whether being chased by a policeman, threatened by fire, or suffering a medical emergency.

It was the perfect object lesson for that time. And since then, as this book demonstrates, I've discovered many more cues to pray. God calls us to live in His presence — praying about *everything*.

It's not *what* we pray that's important. It's *that* we pray. It's *that* we acknowledge God's presence and His involvement in our lives.

And here's a radical idea: *we don't even need words!* When God uses something, anything, even a siren, to remind us that He is there, we can simply sit in silence, enjoying the knowledge that God is with us and that God is with those we're remembering in prayer — especially if their need is urgent. He loves them. He's on the job. He truly cares. *Praise His name!*

Lord, in Hebrews 13:5, we read of Your promise to never leave us or forsake us. Thank You for sending reminders of Your presence every day. Help us to recognize them and take the time to pray.

And thank You for being on the job, responding to life's emergencies even faster than 911 and racing emergency vehicles. Go with them, Lord, providing comfort, help, and healing to those in need. We thank You! Amen.

Praying as Promised

I used to struggle with remembering to pray for specific requests on particular days or at exact times. I sincerely wanted to keep my word to pray if ever I told someone I would, but how easy it is to forget!

My first solution was to whisper a prayer in that moment on the spot, knowing God would remember and honor the prayer. I still try to do this. Then my son Justin offered another solution for when I really want to pray as promised on a certain day. He told me to interrupt a habit. It works like this:

Perhaps a friend is having surgery or going on a job interview. You can remind yourself to pray by putting your watch on your right arm instead of your left. Or you might move your reading glasses to a different shelf, keep your keys in an unusual pocket, or put away all the pens that you leave in strategic locations around the house. (Am I the only one who does that? Surely not.)

Simply move something that you reach for habitually. When you notice it's missing, you'll remember to pray. And if you choose your habit carefully, you'll be praying a lot on that given day.

Father, thank You for the habits that help us organize our lives. And thank You that we can interrupt these habits for such a good purpose. When we notice our subtle sabotage, please remind us to pray. Amen.

Praying over Disagreements

Ever drive yourself crazy trying to get a disagreement out of your mind? The confrontation occurs, yet the person in conflict with you stubbornly refuses to see your point. You find yourself arguing with this person as you go about the business of your day. There's a simple solution! Instead of arguing, pray.

Instead of ranting in your head, pray for anyone who disagrees with you about anything. Whether they are close family, friends, co-workers, or people you've never met whose views you've encountered in the news, pray for these people.

No—you may not pray that God will miraculously change their minds, making them see things *your* way. (But ... but ... but ... —no, you may not. Get over it.)

And no—you may *not* pray that God will zap them with lightning or make their city fall into the sea. (Tempting as it may be, Jesus frowned on this. See Luke 9:54-56.)

Instead:

Pray that God will work His will in their minds and hearts.

Pray that God will bless them abundantly — that they'll find true fulfillment in Him.

Pray that you will have the right attitude toward these people in spite of your differences. Ask God to help you see them through *His* eyes.

They are works in progress, as are you. God loves them dearly; He loves you, too.

Father, when anger and frustration simmer under the surface and try to take over the thoughts in our heads, please remind us to pray. Amen.

Praying the Day's Tragic Headlines

Headlines are full of unspoken prayer requests, so invite God to join you whenever you encounter them. As you read these in your paper or on your homepage or see them on TV, whisper short prayers for the people involved. Pray for victims of natural disasters, their families, and their rescuers. Pray for those injured in vehicle accidents or other mishaps. Pray about crime, trial outcomes, and recovery and restitution for victims.

You may come across local and human interest stories to pray about, too. As you pray for strangers in your city and around the world, God will bring people you know and their personal needs to mind as well. Talk with God about each of these before you go on your way. You're not just keeping yourself informed; you are covering the world in prayer.

Father, whenever we sit down to catch up on the news, please help us view the time as an opportunity to pray. Amen.

Praying for Churches in Headline Areas

I stumbled upon this *Parachute Prayer* while visiting a church in our community that we are blessed to attend from time to time. When the associate pastor stood up to pray, after a great time of worship through song, he took some time to pray for churches located near significant headlines of the previous week. For example, if he were to do that this week, as I'm writing this, he'd pray for churches in Northern California where an earthquake hit, churches in Iraq and Syria where all is in turmoil right now, churches in Ukraine, Russia, Liberia, Iceland . . . you get the idea.

In the previous *Parachute Prayer*, I encouraged you to pray the headlines for those impacted by them, but praying for nearby churches is a great idea, too! We may not be able to go to those places to help, comfort, and encourage, but the people of churches there can and are. And in some cases, they must risk their lives to do so.

When news headlines catch our attention, let's whisper prayers for churches located nearby as we pray for victims, about conflicts, and for all people involved in trying to set things right again.

126

Father, when headlines break our hearts, please call us to pray. We aren't there, but others are. Please use their hands, feet, voices, minds, and hearts to comfort, encourage, and mend as only You can. Amen.

Praying When People Reject God

The Israelites had rejected God as their king, asking instead for a human king like all the other countries had. Without fully realizing their big mistake, they traded the almighty, all-powerful God of the universe for a fallible human hiding behind the baggage.

As God's representative to the Israelites, Samuel felt the sting of their rejection, too. He faced a choice: wash his hands of them entirely or gently point out the mistake, pray for them, and continue to teach as God enabled him to do. Samuel chose to stay, pray, and teach. In fact, he said it would have been a sin not to:

"As for me, far be it from me that I should sin against the Lord by failing to pray for you. And I will teach you the way that is good and right." –1 Samuel 12:23

Today's *Parachute Prayer* is to follow his example. When we're reminded of someone rejecting our amazing, faithful, awesome, unfailing, loving, ever-present God, we can choose to pray. Most likely, we all know someone who has turned from God, breaking our hearts and His, too. We also hear or see headlines everyday about the famous and the infamous who actively deny our Lord. Perhaps whole countries or people groups come to our minds from time to time.

Instead of getting angry and walking away or building a wall to keep those people at bay, let's stay and pray and trust that our lives will teach. As we model what's good and right, covering our world with prayer, people will know, as the Israelites learned, our God is the one true King.

Father, when we learn of people rejecting You, please prompt us immediately to pray. Let our response be one of compassion instead of anger. For the good of Your kingdom, amen.

Praying When We Feel Unlovable

If ever we feel like God is out to get us, 1 Thessalonians 5:9 assures us He's not. In fact, it says God loved us so much that He sent His Son to die for us rather than pour out his anger: "For God chose to save us through our Lord Jesus Christ, not to pour out his anger on us" (NLT). That's love to the *extreme!* God had a choice — and He chose *us!*

In fact, the only way in which God is out to get us, if we haven't already accepted His precious gift of salvation, is to draw us into His perfect kingdom of eternal light and salvation where He can delight in our presence forever as we delight in His!

If that is the case for you, doesn't that make you *want* Him to get you? I'm thankful every day that I am His. You can be His, too. Simply tell Him that you're sorry for your sins, that you want to receive His gift of salvation made available through Christ, and that you will spend the rest of your life learning to know and follow Him, our merciful and gracious, loving God. Welcome to the family! Congratulations on getting got by God!

Along those lines, I have a new *Parachute Prayer*. When we consider the lengths God went to to save us from our sins, we know how precious we are to Him. He created us. He loves us. He invites us to spend eternity with Him—that's a very long time, so He must be absolutely crazy about us in spite of our imperfections and failings! Therefore, whenever we see ourselves in the mirror, we should thank God for making us—fearfully and wonderfully—and for loving us just as we are even on days when we feel unlovable or wonder if anyone else on the planet cares.

And while we're thanking Him for ourselves, we should take the prayer one step further and ask God to help us see ourselves the way He does. I would guess that nobody is harder on a person than that person's self. Thankfully, God is the cure for that. Let's ask Him to show us the truth.

Father, thank You for creating each of us—in Your image and for Your glory! Help us to see ourselves through Your eyes with perfect, loving honesty. Help us to love ourselves as You do, so we can love others more perfectly, too. Amen.

Praying for Those Struggling to Choose Right

At this very moment there are people all over the world who are seriously leaning toward making extreme and desperate choices — painful and permanent decisions that will hurt themselves or others. It's possible we bump elbows with some of these people as we go about the business of a day. It's sobering to realize that we rarely know much of what's on the minds of people even in our own churches, places of business, or crossing our path in the grocery store.

But God knows — and for them, He's given us the privilege to pray. Jesus even taught us to pray, "And lead us not into temptation, but deliver us from the evil one" -Matthew 6:13. Note the plural. The word is *us*. We are to pray for *each other* in this regard. (I know. I know. It's a corporate prayer. But . . . isn't that the point?)

Since arrows indicate direction, let's attach this *Parachute Prayer* to them. When you see a directional arrow, pray that people struggling with temptation will see the way out and make right choices. Ask that God will help them see clearly and give them peace and strength, hope, love, and life.

Father, please bless all who are contemplating making a hurtful choice. Help them to see clearly through their pain and beyond their struggle to the consequences that they won't want to face should they choose to do the wrong thing. Show them the better way – Your way – and give them the strength to move in that direction with hope and peace. Thank You for loving them. Please help them today. Amen.

Praying for Those Who Feel Forgotten

I know some people don't believe in the power of blanket prayers, but, under the right circumstances, I do. Sometimes *we* don't know the specifics, but God *always knows*. When we know the specifics, we should pray for them. Yet if God calls us to pray, even for something that seems generic, we should pray the blanket prayer.

Here's one penned by St. Francis of Assisi that I encourage you to pray often:

"Accept my prayers, dear Father, for those who have no one to love them enough to pray for them. Wherever and whoever they are, give them a share of my blessings, and in thy love let them know that they are not forgotten."

Amen! In the spirit of the *Parachute Prayer*, let's attach this prayer to something that will bring it to mind often. Whenever you see something lost or out of place—like a missing button or a single sock—whisper a prayer for those who have no one else to pray for them.

And don't forget to pray for those who appear to be homeless whenever you see them. They make this blanket prayer a little more specific. No matter what painful circumstance led them into that situation, the homeless anywhere need our prayers.

Father, please help us to notice what's out of place, so we'll remember to pray for those who feel displaced. We may not know who we are praying for, but these just might need prayer most of all. Amen.

Praying for Special Events

I was a nervous wreck when my youngest son took the ACT. Yikes! Such a major exam! I scattered #2 pencils about the house to remind me to pray all morning. Not that I would have forgotten. Just walking by his bedroom door or seeing his picture on the shelf reminded me to whisper prayers that day. But, when something's important to my kids, I want to be sure I remember to pray.

When big events roll around for family members or friends, events we care about but can't attend, symbolic reminders can help us send extra *Parachute Prayers* God's way on their behalf. Exams, sporting or social events, meetings . . . when we want to remember to pray, setting little symbols in odd places where we'll encounter them often will remind us constantly.

Father, when the prayer request is urgent, help us to think strategically. Please give us clever ideas that will remind us we need to pray. Amen.

Praying for People on the Fringe

We all know people who claim to be Christians but don't live like they are following Jesus Christ. Ultimately, the issue is between these people and God. It's not our place to decide who is going to Heaven and who is not. I'm thankful for that! Aren't you? He knows what we do not.

But He has given us guidelines in His Word to help us discern truth. His Spirit dwelling inside gives us wisdom, too. So when we realize that someone who claims to know Christ isn't really living His way, we can recognize this observation as a call to pray.

Growing up, I heard grown-ups in my church refer to these as "fringe" people. Fringe people were loosely associated with the church; they attended once in a while and were somewhat attached to the Body, but they would often disappear—like a frayed thread working its way off of a garment.

Let's use that term for our *Parachute Prayer* prompt. When we see fringes or frayed edges on blankets or clothing, let's stop and pray for people we've wondered about. When we pray, we'll respectfully acknowledge that they claim to be saved children of God. We'll tell God what concerns us, though, and turn our observations over to Him, knowing that He's already aware. We'll ask Him to give us wisdom as we interact with these people; we'll also ask for a double portion of His love to share. Then we'll ask God to help them grow stronger in His knowledge and love each day — from whatever point they're currently at on their spiritual journey.

Father, only You know where the fringe people we care about really stand. We entrust them to Your care. We'll love them in Your name. Please remind us to pray for their spiritual growth whenever You bring thoughts of them into our minds. Amen.

Praying for the Persecuted

While it's true that North Americans may experience some measure of persecution on a small scale, few will ever really know what it means to suffer for Jesus. I can't even begin to fathom how this is possible, but in some countries, what you believe or don't believe can actually be a crime punishable by death or imprisonment. In some countries, Christian parents are declared unfit and have their children taken from them. In some countries, teenagers who choose to follow Christ are disowned and thrown out of their homes onto the streets or turned in to the authorities for arrest. Such things are beyond my comprehension–how people could be so cruel! And yet, some are. Christians really do die for their faith every day.

So let's get in the habit of praying for this suffering part of the Body daily. Here's how we can do that:

Most of us, I think, have some kind of physical quirk that perhaps causes us pain from time to time. (If you don't, be thankful! Then call on your own creative nature to come up with a reminder of your own for this prayer.) For me, the quirk is a shoulder twinge brought on by stress. It's no big deal, just something that prompts me to exercise regularly. Now it will also remind me to pray! You can let your physical quirk be your reminder, too. When we feel a little pain in our physical bodies, let's pray for those members of the Body of Christ who truly are suffering in Jesus' name.

Father, our hearts break when we read about our brothers and sisters in Christ who are being persecuted for serving You. Please give them strength to stand firm in their faith. Please build them up physically and spiritually. Please let them know that You are with them; comfort them as only You can. And please let them know, somehow, that there are people in this world who also care. Bless them, Lord, as You have promised to. Thank You for seeing and honoring their pain. Amen.

Praying for People in Potential Danger

Several years ago, I was lying on the couch reading a great book when my middle son came running through the room with rapid speed. Our small dog was close on his heels, obviously playing "It" in a serious game of tag. Before Windsor could latch on to Alex's pant leg, however, Alex hopped up on a wooden chair. I watched in horror as the chair tilted from its usual 90-degree angle to less than 45. I'm pretty sure there's a law of physics that says a chair pushed to that angle by a fast-moving boy will fall to the floor, carrying the boy with it. To make things worse, the corner of our entertainment center was in the direct path of the boy's forehead, our TV in line with his shoulder. Catastrophe was inevitable; we were headed to the ER.

The accident never happened, though. I was shocked! As I watched, the chair. just. . stopped. . . moving.

Alex froze in place, looking like a surfer holding himself upright at the top of the perfect wave; then he slowly leaned backward to right the chair. As its legs touched the floor, a big, excited grin spread across my son's face as he looked at me, his eyes wide with delight.

"Wasn't that *cool?!*" he said.

I honestly didn't know whether to clap or cry. I couldn't stop a smile of incredulity from spreading across my face, but I did have the presence of mind to show Alex what could have happened, what should have happened, and why he'd better never come that close to making that happen again. When the Bible tells about the work of God's angels, I know it's telling the truth. I haven't actually seen them, but I've seen the results of their actions. I'm thankful God sometimes chooses to send them to protect and care.

The resulting *Parachute Prayer*: When we see small children playing in our neighborhoods or grown-ups doing dangerous jobs such as trimming trees or completing construction projects up high, let's ask God to command His angels to watch over them, to keep them safe from harm.

Father, thank You for the unseen angels who follow Your orders on our behalf. In a world full of danger, their presence is a comfort to us from You. Amen.

Praying Because Some Things Are Imminent

A few years ago, my youngest son and I, like so many others, spent quite a bit of time watching news about the then-recent events in Japan: first, the third largest earthquake in known history, then a tsunami, and finally an explosion or two or three at a nuclear power plant. As the world waited for word of a meltdown, newscasters often used the word, *imminent.*

I didn't understand the complexities or possible consequences of such a thing, yet I knew it was bad. I knew we needed to pray. Moment by moment. For the good of all who were being impacted by those tragic events.

When I was in high school, my family hosted a foreign exchange student from Japan. Her name was Akiko. I don't know where she lives now, but she gave a face to my prayers. I prayed with her in mind as I prayed for everyone over there.

Dictionary.com defines imminent as "likely to occur at any moment; impending." It's an ominous word when you're talking about a nuclear power plant.

As I was thinking about this, I realized that Jesus' return is imminent, too (though I'm not saying that because of Japan's tragedy). Just as news of what was happening in Japan prompted me to pray because of the situation's urgency, knowledge of Jesus' imminent return is a prayer prompt, too. For those of us who live for Him daily, his second coming is something to look forward to. For those who don't know Him, however, His return will be even more catastrophic than events in Japan. Therefore we should find urgency in knowledge of Jesus' coming return, too.

Let's let the word *imminent* prompt us to pray. For those in the midst of a crisis on earth. For the salvation of all who still need to meet Jesus before He returns.

Father, when we learn of imminent danger in our world, please prompt us to pray for those who will be impacted by the event. At the same time, remind us that Jesus' return is also imminent. We must pray for those who don't know You as often as we can. Please draw them into Your kingdom, Lord, for their personal good and for the glory of Your name. Amen.

Praying through the Holidays

Praying for Peace and Unity

The Bible talks a lot about unity. God wants His children, defined here as all of the people He created, to get along. There are children who are living in obedience to Christ, walking with Him faithfully each day. There are children who are living in rebellion against God and His ways. And there are children who haven't yet met our Lord, who don't even know He exists, what He's done for them, or how much He loves them. God wants all of His children to come to know Him and to choose to walk in His ways. He also wants them all to get along.

On Martin Luther King, Jr. Day, we remember this man who dreamed that all people, regardless of race, would someday come to get along. But there are so many other differences that divide. Seems we human beings just begin to come to terms over one of these classifications only to discover another that causes a whole new schism.

I'm thinking this must break God's heart.

Peace and unity are two things we should pray for regularly. Perhaps on a daily basis, we can let controversies and arguments we encounter remind us to pray for these. But let's also set this one day aside for this specific purpose. Throughout the day, whenever we're reminded of Martin Luther King, Jr., let's ask God to help all people learn to set aside their differences and get along—for the sake of our Lord's name.

Father, I'm sorry our conflicts wound You. Thank You for the promise of eternal peace someday. Please help us to work toward that goal now, making every effort, as far as it depends on us, to live at peace. (See Romans 12:18.) Amen.

Worshipping on Valentine's Day

"This is love: not that we loved God, but that he loved us and sent his Son as an atoning sacrifice for our sins." –1 John 4:10

I know Valentine's Day is a greeting card holiday with a focus on romantic love. I have no problem with that. In fact, I enjoy this sweet day. And I always use it as a perfect excuse to shower a little extra love not only on the one romantic interest of my life, my darling husband, but also on my other loves, my precious children. One can never give or receive too many reminders that one is loved!

But the Bible tells us that God Is love. He defines it. He reveals it. He gives it liberally! Therefore He also, above all others, deserves some attention on Valentine's Day.

Throughout this day, whenever we hear the word Valentine, let's offer prayers of devotion to our highest Love. Let's tell Him how much we love Him, how awesome He Is. In other words, let's worship Him today. He gave His only Son to rescue us from sin, so we can spend eternity with Him. Whispering prayers of praise and adoration is the least that we can do. (And it makes Valentine's Day so much more than just another greeting card holiday!)

Father, You are the one we've turned our lives and hearts over to entirely. We love You; we are Yours. Thank You for the gift of salvation and the hope of eternity in Your presence. We're dreaming of that day as we walk through this life with You. Thank You for making our relationship possible and for blessing all of our other relationships in the process. You are worthy of our adoration, worship, and praise. Amen.

Praying on Good Friday

Good Friday. A day to be thankful. A day to mourn—and pray!

Those of us who've invited Jesus to be our Savior don't mourn His death on Good Friday. We know He rose again and lives right now. Hallelujah! He's risen indeed!

We don't mourn our sins on Good Friday either, for we know they've been forgiven and forgotten and drowned in the deepest sea. For that reason, we pray, "Thank You, Jesus, for saving me!"

What we mourn, then, on this thought-provoking, sunny, yet gloomy, yet hopeful Good Friday is all the people out there who haven't yet turned to Christ, those who've heard the good news and rejected it for themselves, those who absolutely and stubbornly refuse to believe. In a sense, they are living in death because their souls haven't been resurrected into new life in Christ. They are missing out on life, and that is sad.

Won't you join me in praying for these lost souls? As we prepare to celebrate the glorious resurrection of our Lord and Savior on Easter day, let's pray for the resurrection of dead hearts all over this world.

Jesus died and rose for everyone! Let's pray many will come to realize this and choose to believe now.

Father, our Jesus is risen! He's risen, indeed! In the midst of our celebration, please remind us to pray for those who refuse to see this truth. Open their hearts, Lord. Please draw them to You. Amen.

Praying Easter Every Day

In the years I've been writing *Parachute Prayers* on my blogs, I've never written one for Easter. I couldn't imagine leaving Easter out of this collection of holiday prayers, though. Yet I struggled to think of an appropriate prayer prompt for this day. Everything seemed trite; nothing was enough.

It finally occurred to me that Easter's *Parachute Prayer* is one we live—every hour of every day. In fact, it's one our Lord Himself gave.

Imagine that. Jesus taught His followers a *Parachute Prayer*! It's one most followers practice regularly:

"The Lord Jesus, on the night he was betrayed, took bread, and when he had given thanks, he broke it and said, 'This is my body, which is for you; do this in remembrance of me.' In the same way, after supper he took the cup, saying, 'This cup is the new covenant in my blood; do this, whenever you drink it, in remembrance of me.' For whenever you eat this bread and drink this cup, you proclaim the Lord's death until he comes." -1 Corinthians 11:23-26

Easter's *Parachute Prayer* is the prayer of remembrance. Whenever we take communion (whatever the day), whenever we eat or drink, whenever we see a cross or a resurrection sunrise or anything that reminds us of all Jesus did for us, we pause to remember. We pray. We praise. We worship. We thank.

And we do this every day because Jesus lives! He lives within us and all around us. He is present, and we are never alone. By acknowledging His presence, recognizing His work in our day-to-day lives, and remembering He Is here, we pray Easter all our days. This is the ultimate *Parachute Prayer*. We owe everything to Christ.

Jesus, we remember. Thank You for all You've done, all You are doing, and all You will do. Remind us often! Call us to pray. We owe all we are to You. Amen.

Praying for Courage on Columbus' Day

Columbus set sail for the new world in faith. The rest of the known world believed that the horizon was the edge of the earth and that sailing too close to it would result in death. Columbus disagreed, but he didn't have proof — only faith.

As we think about Columbus on his day, let's pray for the unknowns of our futures. We can only see so far, and even what we can see is unpredictable. When we think of it, we may feel anticipation or trepidation or both. We can turn these emotions over to God, asking Him to help us move forward courageously with our faith firmly in Him.

Columbus had faith in an idea and things worked out pretty well for him. With our faith placed in our sovereign God, we cannot go wrong.

Father, thank You for Columbus' bold example. Please give us courage to face whatever comes. We know You know what lies ahead. We're sailing with You. Amen.

Praying for Neighbors on Halloween

I think the thing I enjoy most about Halloween is getting to greet all of our neighbors right on our own doorstep. Throughout most of the year, our quiet neighborhood is, well, quiet! We might get to wave at a neighbor or two when taking out the trash or picking up the mail or while out on a walk, but that's about it. On Halloween, though, the neighbors all come out and visit each other. I get to greet the children, tell them how cute or scary or beautiful or funny they are and give them candy which brings smiles to their faces in exchange for the smile they put on my own. I get to say *Hi* to all their parents and wish them a happy evening. I get to laugh as our dog attempts to go home with every child who comes to the door. (He just wants to join in the fun!) Halloween may be known for the scary stuff, but I think it's just a great opportunity for everyone to be extra friendly!

If you're greeting trick-or-treaters this Halloween, remember to whisper brief prayers for them, too. We may pray for our neighbors in general throughout the year, but, on Halloween, we can pray for them specifically as we see their faces, greet them, and offer sweet treats. If you don't participate in this aspect of the day, that's alright. You can still pray for the families you see through your window or hear walking down your street. Your prayers that they'll come to know Jesus, if they don't already, and that they'll grow healthy and strong both physically and spiritually may be the best treat they'll never know they received.

Father, bless all the trick-or-treaters and their families on Halloween night. Keep them safe and help them have good, clean fun. Thank You for this opportunity to see neighbors who usually stay in their homes. Help us remember to pray for them not only on this night, but throughout the year. May they come to know You well then grow in Your love each day. Thank You, Lord! Amen.

Praying Our Masks Away

When I was little, children often wore plastic masks for Halloween. My mother always made my costumes, so I never did, but I did try my friends' masks on. They were so uncomfortable! The edges of the hard plastic scratched my face, the elastic that held the mask in place tangled in my hair, and, inevitably, that elastic snapped and smacked somebody's skin. But we all thought the masks were fun because they let us look like something we weren't.

I'm glad those particular masks are a thing of the past, but kids still dress up on Halloween. This gives us another *Parachute Prayer*.

When we see neighborhood kids in costume, let's ask God to help us identify and remove any non-physical masks we wear daily. There are times when we all pretend to be someone we're not. We act differently than we normally would in order to make a better impression, be accepted, or hide emotional pain.

But God knows all that's true about us, and He loves us dearly. We don't need to impress Him. He will not reject a sincere heart. He sees and is able and willing to heal all emotional pain. We can go to Him just as we are with every big and little thing. And then we can live that relationship before others, so that they can see the truth of what God saw in us, what God did for us, and just how awesome our God is.

Father, whenever we see physical masks on others, please point out any non-physical masks we wear. Teach us to live authentically, so others can see Your truth. Amen.

Praying for Gratitude on Thanksgiving

A few Thanksgivings back, I tried something new that seemed corny at first yet became meaningful to me. I look forward to doing this again each year now. Here is the idea:

I had become overwhelmed with meal preparation and household décor and all the details of creating the perfect Thanksgiving Day when I realized my attitude was anything but thankful. I didn't want that. God didn't want that. Nobody wanted that! One cannot create the perfect meal if one is frazzled. Food should be presented with grace, not grumpiness.

To adjust my mental state, I slipped away for a while, grabbed my journal and a pen, and began to pray. Because it was Thanksgiving Day, giving thanks seemed to be the most appropriate prayer, so I began listing anything and everything I could think of to be thankful for—from the carpet under my feet, to the warm throw wrapped around my shoulders, to my precious family, to God's Spirit guiding my thoughts, to the air I was breathing. Big things, little things—it was a brainstorm of thanksgiving.

Since a list like that could go on and on, you may want to set a timer when you pray this *Parachute Prayer*. Make a game of thanking God for everything you can think of in 5, 10 or 15 minutes. Or maybe, start your Thanksgiving list the Sunday before, continue some on Monday and the next day and so on all week long. Your goal is to generate a true spirit of thankfulness in your heart, to not take anything for granted, but to realize it all comes from God — your life, your salvation, your family, your home, your community, this planet, toothpaste, toe nail clippers, and the tree outside your door.

As we get ready to celebrate Thanksgiving Day, let's prepare our hearts by filling them with thanksgiving first. Then, as we enjoy our Thanksgiving meals, let's offer God all the thanks we've stored up.

Father, as we enjoy the day especially set aside for this practice, help us to truly practice being thankful. Then please let memories of this stick with us throughout the year. Thanksgiving is something You deserve to receive each day. Amen.

Praying for God's Harvest at Thanksgiving

"Then he said to his disciples, 'The harvest is plentiful but the workers are few. Ask the Lord of the harvest, therefore, to send out workers into his harvest field.'" –Matthew 9:37-38

What a perfect verse for November when we're surrounded by reminders of the harvest—apples, pumpkins, Thanksgiving décor! As we prepare for Thanksgiving, these remind us to give thanks for all God has provided all year long.

But though I *am* eternally thankful, I am also concerned about the harvest Jesus was referring to. There are people out there who have much, yet without Jesus, don't really have anything. There are people who have little and need Jesus, too.

Jesus says there are plenty of hearts out there ready to receive all He has to give—ready to be brought into the Kingdom of God—ready to celebrate Thanksgiving completely, not only for what they have but also for salvation and a life with Jesus, too. So when we see signs of harvest, let's pray as Jesus told His disciples to! Let's pray that He'll send workers into His harvest field who will faithfully lead ready hearts to Him.

And while we're at it, let's not forget to ask Him to show us what *we* can do. We may be just the workers He needs to reach those near our homes for Him. We may be the very workers He's asked us to pray He'll send.

Lord of the Harvest, please send many workers into Your field. The harvest is plentiful; call Your people to bring it in. Make each of us open to what You're leading us to do. We know You'll help us because You love those who are waiting in the field. Thank You, Lord! May this year's harvest be the best one yet! Amen.

Praying for People Who Don't Feel Thankful

Though Thanksgiving is a time set aside for giving thanks to God for all He's given us, I know with certainty that there are many people among us right now who are struggling to do this—if they're even trying at all. Some are grieving. Some are lonely. Some are desperately in need. Some suffer from depression. For whatever reason, they just aren't feeling thankful, and, though people can offer thanks to God whether their emotions are involved or not, this is a choice they must wrestle through, one that requires great trust and determination. It's one that many give up on or refuse by settling for bitterness. As we give thanks for our blessings this week, let's boost these people with prayer.

And since we're praying for people who aren't feeling thankful, let's let the most unthankful one in our midst remind us to pray for these. When we see our Thanksgiving turkey (or ham), let's remember that not everyone gets to enjoy a happy Thanksgiving. We make jokes about the poor turkey's sacrifice, but it is a sacrifice just the same—and we're thankful for it as we enjoy our dinner with all the fixings!

When God gives us reason to celebrate, we honor Him by doing so with all our heart—especially at Thanksgiving. We're thanking Him by enjoying the blessings He's provided, by inviting Him to be present, the Guest of Honor at our feast. But we honor Him even more when we remember in the midst of our fun that some aren't experiencing it. Let's take time to pray for their needs.

Father, Thanksgiving is a curious thing. It's a matter of the heart really. On this day, You will watch as some of the most wealthy grumble and complain while some of the most impoverished thank You for whatever they can all day (and the other way around). Circumstance isn't what enables us to give thanks. So please help people who are struggling to be thankful to find reason for gratitude. Even the turkey, if turkeys could be thankful, might be grateful to discover the purpose of his sacrifice. You created him to feed someone hungry, to be the main course at a meal that honors You.

And Father, as those who are struggling to be thankful wrestle with this, please send comfort their way. You care about heart attitudes, but You also care about circumstances. Please provide what Your people need. Encourage them on their way. Let them know that You are the God Who sees and that You are taking care of them always. For this and so much more, we thank You, Lord. Amen.

Praying Memories at Christmas

Every Christmas tree is unique. I know this. Some are carefully planned, designer decorated. Others have brightly colored lights, ribbons, glass ornaments, angels or birds. Some are probably *Hallmark* through and through. Ours is chaos! But we love it for that—in some ways, you could say, it's a memory tree.

There are several types of ornaments on our tree. First there are the ornaments we received as wedding gifts. (When you get married at Christmastime, you start off with quite a collection.) Each of these reminds me of a precious wedding guest.

Then there are the ornaments the boys made in school and Sunday school through their preschool and elementary years. These trigger memories of favorite teachers and Christmases past.

We also have ornaments from each of the places where we've lived: Delft ornaments from the Netherlands, an armadillo wearing a Santa hat from Texas, a lobster from Maine that's decorated in holly.

And finally there are the gifts from friends and co-workers we've met along the way. Every time I see the Ohio-shaped cookie cutter decorated with red and green ribbons and little silver bells, I remember the friend who gave it to me. She was right; that unique ornament will always remind me of her and from whence she came.

Whether or not you have a tree of memories, certain elements of Christmas are bound to send your thoughts into the past. When you find yourself reminiscing, whisper a prayer for the person or group who visits your mind. Let's offer Christmas prayers to God as gifts for the people we've known and loved throughout our lives.

Father, You've blessed us with precious memories. Help us to use them as reminders to pray for the people you've brought to touch our lives. Amen.

Praying Inspired by Christmas Cards

As time marches on and technology changes, it seems more and more likely that Christmas cards may someday become a part of history. I still love them, though, and am thankful for those I receive. I'm thankful for greetings that come by e-mail and social media, too, but there's just something special about a message enclosed in a work of art that I can hold in my hands. (I guess that tells you how I feel about books and photo albums, too.)

Here are a few *Parachute Prayers* inspired by Christmas cards:

1. As we address the cards (or enter e-mail addresses into our message's "send to" line), let's pray for the families who live in those homes (or who use those computers). Let's especially ask God to help these precious people experience His presence during the holiday. Let's ask His blessings on the events of their coming year.

2. Let's pray again as we receive cards or replies.

3. Let's keep our Christmas cards through the coming year and pray for a different family (represented by the card they sent) each week or each night, as we can, or simply draw a card from the pile

randomly from time to time, saying a prayer on the sender's behalf.

As we pray, we'll be doing more than simply enjoying those beautiful Christmas cards—we'll be using them to bless others throughout the whole next year.

Father, as we send and receive Christmas greetings, please remind us to pray. The people we remember and who remember us at Christmas are precious gifts from You. We ask You now to bless them every day. Amen.

Praying While We Wrap Presents

As we entered the Christmas season one year, I found myself in a quandary. I was reading through Ephesians and the Kings. How was I to contemplate Christmas? I considered saving those books for January, so I could turn to Matthew and Luke. But then I read Ephesians 1 and realized God has scattered Christmas messages throughout His whole Word!

Many of us teach our children that we give gifts at Christmas to remember God's great Christmas Gift to us — the Baby, Jesus Christ, who came to save us from our sins. Ephesians 1 makes this clear — especially in verses 7-8: "In him we have redemption through his blood, the forgiveness of sins, in accordance with the riches of God's grace that he lavished on us." In Jesus, God, the Father, gave us a *lavish* gift of grace.

Don't you just love that word? *Lavish.* I picture grace spilling out all over the place, dripping from the branches of the Christmas tree, covering the floor, and moving right into the next room of the house — or maybe from our souls into all others we meet. *Wow!*

As we wrap gifts for loved ones, we joyfully anticipate the looks on their faces. We carefully choose gifts we hope they'll love and appreciate because we love them *so much!* Imagine our loving Father God doing the same — tenderly giving a precious newborn to His handmaiden, Mary, then sending hosts of angels to deliver the happy message that the Gift has arrived for the all the world to worship and enjoy!

Oh, come let us adore Him indeed!

As we wrap presents each Christmas, let's reflect on God's lavish gift of grace. Then let's pray that the person we are giving something to will have *at least* one poignant moment of realization this season of God's offered redemption, forgiveness, and lavishly rich, given grace.

Thank You, Father, for Your Lavish Christmas Gift. Thank You for Jesus. Thank You for redemption and forgiveness. Thank You for Grace. Please help our loved ones to enjoy and appreciate these this season, too — and all through their lives. We love You. We want them to love You more and more thoroughly, too. Amen.

Praying While Baking for Christmas

As my sons became teenagers, my Christmas baking had to change. Instead of carefully frosted sugar cookies, my new holiday favorite became *Laura Bush's Cowboy Cookies*. We just dumped everything in the bowl, mixed it up, dropped it on the cookie sheet, and baked. No more rebellious boys reshaping the camels to do aerobics instead of walk to Bethlehem. No more digging fragile angel wings out of forgotten-to-be-floured cookie cutters. No more flour all over my kitchen. No more being left alone to frost a zillion sugar cookies all by myself as my mutinous elves got bored and slunk off to play elsewhere.

My teenage boys had better things to do than frost cookies.

Don't get me wrong. I *love* baking sugar cookies! I just needed a year or two or three to recover from ambitiously trying to bake too many and traumatizing the whole family with the result. I *really* love baking sugar cookies—but, I suppose, a batch or two would have been enough.

The boys *emphatically* agreed.

Still, many of us go overboard when it comes to baking and food preparation at Christmas. So let's add one element to make the task even more rewarding. Let's involve our hearts and minds with prayer:

As we add ingredients, let's think about where they came from, thank God for them, pray for the farmers who grew them, processors who prepared and packaged them, and grocers who sold them to us. Let's pray for self-control, that we won't overindulge—too much! Then let's pray for those who don't have such luxuries as cookies and pies and Christmas hams and yams and potatoes and cranberry sauce—the jellied kind, of course. As you wipe flour off your table and frosting off the ceiling, pray for those who'll never experience such *fun!* Then pray for those who did—with you—even if they did slink off to play before the job was done.

Father, we are so blessed to be able to bake for Christmas fun. As we do, remind us to pray with thanksgiving for all You've given and with love for everyone involved. Amen.

Praying for Families Separated at Christmas

Once upon a time, when my husband was deployed to Iraq over Christmas, I found myself reduced to a puddle of tears right in the middle of the baking goods aisle at WalMart by Karen Carpenter's beloved song, *Merry Christmas, Darling*, playing throughout the store.

As the season progressed, I didn't fare much better with Elvis's, *Blue Christmas*, or the ever-popular, *I'll Be Home for Christmas*, playing at the mall or anywhere.

Bah, humbug.

I remember thinking at the time that playing these songs was a bit cruel. I'd like to formally request that all merchants nationwide stick to playing cheerful Christmas music in public places this season of the year. No offense meant to Karen, Elvis, or any other Christmas crooners.

Alas, I don't have much faith in the power of one book to change the playlists of shopping centers across the country. So I'll suggest a more positive twist:

When we hear these songs while Christmas shopping, let's pray for military families who can't be together for the holidays. Who knows? The lady one aisle over may be frantically trying to bury her tears in a bag of brown sugar. Ask God to cheer her heart, keep her husband safe, and happily reunite them *soon*.

Father, it's nice to be together at Christmas, but sometimes it just isn't possible. Please encourage families who have to be apart. Remind them of their purpose. Assure them their sacrifice is not in vain. And help them to find creative and meaningful ways to celebrate together by heart, if not by locale. Comfort them, Lord, as only You can. Thank You, Jesus! Amen.

Praying for Holiday Travelers

As we all know, the Christmas holidays are the busiest times of year for travel. Someone near and dear to my heart is living his own version of *Planes, Trains, and Automobiles* as I type this. If you're preparing for the winter holidays as you read this, you probably know someone in the same boat — or should I say airplane? The busiest weeks of the year for travel just happen to coincide with some of the worst weeks of winter, making travel a truly grand adventure country-wide. So, remind me again, who said dreaming of a white Christmas was such a great idea?

Throughout the holiday season, as we see airplanes flying overhead or as we drive over railroad tracks or even stop for red lights, let's breathe a prayer for travelers everywhere. Let's pray for those who are moving from point A to point B, for those who serve them in the air or on the ground, and for those who wait at home, eagerly anticipating a happy holiday reunion. And while we're at it, let's pray that those reunions truly will be joyful, blessed times for all.

Father, please bless the travelers — as You blessed Mary and Joseph when they traveled to Bethlehem so long ago. May today's travelers reflect on that time and relate thankfully as they make their way to their own Christmas destinations. Bless the travel industry workers with patience and wisdom; please provide safe weather and seating for all. And encourage the families and friends who wait — remind them to pray as they do. May reunions be joyful as people gather to celebrate You this year! Amen.

Praying about How We See Ourselves

As we prepare for each new year, whether we make resolutions or not, many of us become introspective, considering improvements, goals, habits, and dreams. There's just something about a new day, week, month, year, decade, or millennium that seems to trigger this in us: the desire to grab hold of something brand new and make something beautiful out of it.

I think it has something to do with being made in the image of our grand, Creator God. We want to create, too! Yet when one year doesn't go exactly as planned, we look forward to the opportunity to try all over again.

I don't usually make resolutions, but I do set goals, make plans, and dream. If you approach the New Year this way, too, you need to know that all this introspection, reflection, and goal-setting is meaningless if your perspective is off. In order to move forward effectively, we must first learn to see ourselves as God sees us.

For example, whether or not we lose an extra five pounds is probably one of God's lower priorities for us. He wants us to make healthy choices and care for

His design. If we're doing that, the number on the scale is irrelevant. When we train ourselves to place our focus where His is — such as on the healthy choice instead of on the scale— we'll probably take a lot of pressure off of ourselves. Then we will be able to serve Him with a better frame of mind: "God loves me and has meaningful work for me to do. I'll care for myself so that I can serve Him well," rather than "I'm not good enough to serve God because I just can't seem to reach this goal. I am a failure. I'm incompetent. Poor me."

In light of this, let's practice a new *Parachute Prayer*: Whenever you see your reflection, pray, *"Father, please help me see myself as You see me. Help me to cooperate with You as I see You working in my life. Make me over in Your image that I'll be able to serve You well. Amen."*

If we do this, God will answer our prayer and help us to see our own lives from His perspective which is, truthfully, the only perspective that counts. Armed with this point of view, we'll be able to step into any new year with confidence.

Father, when we see our reflections in the mirror, please remind us at this introspective time of year that

Your opinion of us is the one that counts. Remind us to ask You to help us see ourselves as You do and to humbly cooperate with the improvements in our selves that You are striving to make. Amen.

Praying on Loved Ones' Birthdays

As I'm writing this today, it is someone's birthday. I won't mention her by name. I wouldn't want to embarrass her or anything. But she is on my mind, and I feel prompted to pray.

So, as I send her gift, I'll whisper a prayer, thanking God for her life and asking Him to bless her throughout this next year — and *always!*

Then I will remember, as I always do, that I have a cousin her same age. I'll pray for him, too.

Then I'll think of all the people in our family who have a birthday in this month. It seems just about everyone in our extended family on my mother's side either has a birthday in this month or has a spouse, child, or parent with a birthday in this month. If you're part of our family, you're planning a party now!

Once I've remembered all the birthdays, I'll probably go on to think of the crazy couple who decided to get married in the midst of all these birthdays adding an anniversary to the celebration parade. I'll pray that God will add many blessings to this precious marriage, too.

It seems a birthday can trigger all kinds of *Parachute Prayers*! What a great opportunity to ask God's blessing on our families and friends.

Father, thank You for each life we celebrate on a happy birthday — or anniversary! Please bless those we love through the coming year and always with health, with love, and with a growing knowledge of You. Amen.

Praying Anywhere

Praying Praises

"Praise the Lord. How good it is to sing praises to our God, how pleasant and fitting to praise him!" – Psalm 147:1

While most *Parachute Prayers* are intercessory, Psalm 147 is a beautiful example of *Parachute Praise*. In this especially beautiful psalm, the psalmist first commands his readers to praise the Lord and then tells them *why*: it's *good* to sing praises to God; it's *pleasant and fitting* to praise Him! The psalmist follows this declaration with a comprehensive brainstorm of praise:

"The Lord builds up Jerusalem;
   he gathers the exiles of Israel.
He heals the brokenhearted
   and binds up their wounds.
He determines the number of the stars
   and calls them each by name.
Great is our Lord and mighty in power;
   his understanding has no limit.
The Lord sustains the humble
   but casts the wicked to the ground . . .

He covers the sky with clouds;
  he supplies the earth with rain
  and makes grass grow on the hills.
He provides food for the cattle
  and for the young ravens when they call.
His pleasure is not in the strength of the horse,
  nor his delight in the legs of the warrior;
the Lord delights in those who fear him,
  who put their hope in his unfailing love . . .
He strengthens the bars of your gates
  and blesses your people within you.
He grants peace to your borders
  and satisfies you with the finest of wheat.
He sends his command to the earth;
  his word runs swiftly.
He spreads the snow like wool
  and scatters the frost like ashes.
He hurls down his hail like pebbles.
  Who can withstand his icy blast?
He sends his word and melts them;
  he stirs up his breezes, and the waters flow.
He has revealed his word to Jacob,
  his laws and decrees to Israel.
He has done this for no other nation;
  they do not know his laws.

Praise the Lord."

Now let's use Psalm 147:1 to trigger our own *Parachute Praise*! Write the words out on an index card and place it somewhere appropriate. For example, laminate it and tape it to an outdoor table, so you'll see it when you go outside. Or place it inside your prayer journal where you'll see it whenever you sit down to pray. Wherever you place it, when you see it, spend a few moments brainstorming praises like the Psalmist did. You may even choose to memorize the verse, so God's Spirit can use it to launch a random praise session from your heart anytime. Our Creator, Teacher, Savior, Father God is worthy of more praise than words exist to offer it to Him. Like the psalmist, let's praise Him often — and *comprehensively!*

Father, as we whisper prayers throughout the day, remind us to include many that offer praise to You. Amen.

Praying D.E.A.P.ly

Two of the school systems that my children have been part of over the years have used an idea called D.E.A.R.: Drop Everything and Read. At a certain time of each school day, everyone in the school, administrators, secretaries, and the school nurse included, dropped whatever he or she was doing in order to read for 15 minutes. Each child had a library book or favorite reading book from home available for this purpose. When the bell rang for D.E.A.R., everyone in the building stopped working to read. Once in a while, I played too, enjoying knowing that my kids and I were doing the same thing, though I was home and they were at school.

I like the D.E.A.R. concept. It shows the kids that reading can be fun and relaxing, not just schoolwork, and that adults enjoy reading, too. It allows the kids to choose their own reading materials for a portion of the day, and for that time, everyone in the building unites to participate in the same activity, even though each is reading alone.

So let's call today's *Parachute Prayer*, D.E.A.P: Drop Everything and Pray. (I know I'm spelling deep wrong, but I'm willing to overlook that for the sake of the idea.) To start, choose a time of day for every day, setting an alarm if you need to. When the chosen time rolls around, simply drop whatever you're doing and pray. Consider inviting your family to pray at the same time, so that, wherever you are, whatever you're doing, for a time, you'll all be united in prayer.

As reading is D.E.A.R. (Ooh—could we adapt that for Bible reading time?), prayer is D.E.A.P., drawing us into a deeper relationship with Christ. Let's plan to take a break each day— drop *everything*—to talk with our great God.

Father, help us choose a time and stick with it. We want to develop the happy habit of talking with You each day. Amen.

Praying as Thoughts Connect

Sometimes when Mike and I are talking, there will be a comfortable and thoughtful lull in the conversation. In the quiet, my mind will jump from the topic we're discussing to another, then rapidly to another and another. I may say something about the topic my mind moves to.

Confused, Mike will ask, "How did we go from talking about this to talking about that?" The transition seems obvious and seamless to me, but Mike can't read my mind. To him the new topic is random and unrelated. For the fun of it, I'll backtrack and verbally walk Mike through the steps my thoughts took to get from Topic A to Topic B. Then we'll laugh at the interesting connections our minds sometimes make.

These random mind transitions don't just happen between Mike and me. They're a part of every conversation. Our minds work faster than our mouths and make unvoiced connections as we talk. When one person's brain goes one way and the other's another, the conversation can get confusing. It's fun to ask, "Where did that thought come from?" and then to analyze.

Today's *Parachute Prayer* uses these thought connections. The conversation is between you and God. He *can* read your mind, though, and since you're praying, His Spirit will probably be guiding your thoughts.

To begin, grab a pencil and a piece of paper (*required*). Then find a quiet place to pray. Talk to God about the first person, activity, event, or place that comes to mind. Write one or two words on your piece of paper to represent the subject of your prayer. As you're praying, your mind will jump to another person, activity, event, or place. Write it down and pray. Continue to pray this way for as long as you like, until you sense the conversation is coming to its natural close. Think of it as a new kind of prayer chain—a chain of thought, rather than of people praying.

Sometimes your mind will produce a rapid succession of names—a list of people with health concerns, perhaps. Write them all down, breathing quick prayers as you do. Other times, your mind may linger on one very specific need—maybe an upcoming ministry event with many details you can cover in prayer. Devote as much time to this one thing as you feel compelled to; you may even turn your paper over to journal a prayer before returning to your list. When your mind jumps to something else, move on.

Close by thanking God for His guidance, His sovereignty, and His loving care.

Praying this way, you may find yourself praying for what you never thought you would, what wouldn't have occurred to you otherwise. Yet you'll truly be sending out those parachutes that God will faithfully use to bless and better this world, building His Kingdom "in earth, as it is in Heaven" (Matthew 6:10, KJV).

Father, guide our thoughts to expand the reach of our prayers. We long to help You bless this world by preparing all hearts for the next. Amen.

Praying by Accident

"She found herself praying . . ."

I came across this phrase in a novel I was reading and thought it was so profound. How fun to find yourself praying when you aren't even meaning to, at a time when you least expect to be talking to God — yet there you are in whatever unlikely place with whichever unlikely people breathing soft prayers to your Lord.

I'm not sure this really fits the definition of a *Parachute Prayer* because those are kinda, sorta, somewhat intentional. *Parachute Prayers* are whispered on specific cues. Yet sometimes those cues catch us unexpectedly, and we find ourselves praying before we realize that that's what we're doing. So this *Parachute Prayer* is a challenge to catch ourselves doing just that!

If you've never *found* yourself praying before, you can actually train for this. Set times to pray intentionally throughout your day. You can even use ideas from some of the other *Parachute Prayers*, letting objects and events around you remind you to pray. As you spend more time *intentionally* talking to God, you'll notice His Spirit calling you to pray at other times, too. When you sense this call to prayer, you'll act on it. Eventually, you'll find yourself praying like the lady in the novel did. Talking to God will be the natural thing to do.

Father, please remind us to keep on practicing prayer, experiencing Your presence constantly in our lives. Teach us to talk to You about everything, everywhere, all the time. You are with us. We know this, and so we'll talk with You. Amen.

Praying Away Worries

A persistent worry can be as annoying as the song that gets stuck in my head. No matter how badly I want to quit listening, it just keeps playing, ever more loudly as it circles around my mind. I know that worry shows a lack of trust in God's ability to handle the troubles of my life, so I want to rid myself of the worrisome thought and show my trust in God. I want to obediently turn all my worries over to him. Yet some worries seem to have a life of their own, a will to come back whether I want them or not. What's a girl to do but cover her ears and shout, "Lord, make it stop!"?

That's exactly what a girl's to do. Colossians 4:2 tells us to devote ourselves to prayer. When worry won't be silent, we can rewrite it as a *Parachute Prayer*:

> *Father, this problem is persistent. I can't get it out of my mind, so I'll use it as a cue to pray, again and again, as long as it takes. You are more powerful than this worry. Please work out all the details according to Your perfect will.*

As we rewrite the worry, we'll become thankful for its cue. The worry becomes a reminder to pray, an affirmation of God's sovereignty, and an opportunity to develop trust in the one who loves us like no one else can. And so we pray with gratitude, and then we watch. God's gonna work, and His solution is gonna be great!

Father, I'm watching. Take my worry and turn it into something that honors You! Amen.

Praying as They Go and We Arrive

I have two, closely-related *Parachute Prayers* for you today. The first comes from a long-time habit of mine. Whenever a family member leaves the house, I watch from the window until he drives from sight. Knowing where this person is going, I can pray for him and about the planned activity, whatever it is. (I can also pray for his safety.) That's today's *Parachute Prayer* #1: When family members leave the house, we can watch them go and pray.

The second is for ourselves. When we go to events such as Bible study, meetings, coffees, and such, we can pray for ourselves and the event, whatever it is, as we walk from our cars to the building. We can pray for friends who will be there, about topics we'll be studying or discussing, for teachers, speakers, leaders, and participants. We can thank God for His Presence and ask for His blessing. *Parachute Prayer* #2: When we attend events, we can walk in and pray.

Father, it's good to pray about events we and our loved ones will be attending. As we watch them go and as we go on our way, please remind us to use that time to pray. Amen.

Praying What We Hear

Whenever I run on my treadmill, like so many other runners, I set my MP3 player to shuffle and listen to whatever comes on. First up one morning a few years ago, it chose Huey Lewis's *Heart of Rock & Roll*. (How'd that get on my machine?)

Okay, I confess. I put it there—but the music I run to must have a beat. You can't run 5 miles to quiet praise and worship songs that call you to drop to your knees. In fact, on your treadmill, you could end up in the hospital that way! And so, tucked in among all my favorite upbeat contemporary Christian artists are a few older, but fun groups like *Huey Lewis and the News*. (Just don't ask me to tell who else you may find there. The *Go-Go's* are none of your business!)

Anyway, as Huey was singing about New York and Los Angeles and so many other American cities where the Heart of Rock & Roll is alive and well, I heard him mention Boston and remembered the marathon . . . and the attacks that had happened that week. Then he mentioned Oklahoma City, and I remembered the headline I'd seen that very morning about tornadoes hitting there . . . again. And as I ran

198

and listened, I prayed. (You can't run and kneel, but you *can* run and pray — with eyes open, please.)

That's what *Parachute Prayers* are all about — letting the Holy Spirit use anything, anywhere, anytime remind you to pray for those who need a touch from God in the moment, this moment, right now.

(Incidentally, *The Go-Go's* reminded me to pray Psalm 19:14 for myself and others: May the words of my mouth be acceptable in Your sight, Lord — or else, let my lips be sealed!)

Father, as we go about the business of our day, keep our ears open to words, whether encased in music or not, that will remind us to pray for the people in our world who need Your touch in a special way today. Amen.

Praying when Tears Come to Our Eyes

"He will wipe away every tear from their eyes, and death shall be no more, neither shall there be mourning, nor crying, nor pain anymore, for the former things have passed away." -Revelation 21:4, ESV

I love this verse simply because of the hope it gives. Someday the circumstances that cause us to grieve, cry, or suffer pain, whether physical or emotional, will cease to exist. And God Himself will wipe the last tears from our eyes. We need to remember this because in this world, we do have trouble and, sometimes, it causes us to mourn, cry, and feel pain.

For this reason, I'd like to suggest this verse as a trigger for *Parachute Prayer*. When tears come to our eyes, whether through our own hurts, out of compassion for someone else's, or even because of a moving story in a book or movie, let's pause to consider Revelation 21:4 and to thank God for what He promises to do someday. As we place our hope in Him, He'll comfort us even now. That's a truth worth remembering.

Father, thank You for the promise of Heaven. I look forward to seeing Your face to face someday. I wonder if those last tears You wipe from our eyes will be tears of joy at finding hope fulfilled forever at last! Amen.

Praying Our Way through Brick Walls

We've all had days where everything we try to do goes wrong. Other times, we schedule baby steps toward reaching big goals: "I'll do this by this date, then this by this date, then this by this date," and so on. But brick walls appear just before each little goal, hindering our progress . . . causing much frustration.

Today's *Parachute Prayer* is to pray when brick walls block our way. It's hard, I know. But on a bad day when all's going wrong, dropping everything to ask God for wisdom, assistance, even blessing not only comforts us but also often helps us to find a better way.

Who knows? Maybe the brick wall is something to be thankful for. Maybe God has a different plan for our day. Maybe God is challenging our commitment or using the obstacle to strengthen our resolve. If we don't talk to Him about it, we'll never know — and we may never reach our goals. We'll just get many bruises from throwing ourselves at the immovable, go to bed exhausted, and have to face it all again another day. When obstacles confound us, it's worth our time to stop and pray.

Father, please help us to remember You in the midst of our frustration, so that we'll pause to pray. You're probably waiting for us to do just that. You have the wisdom that we lack; please turn our thoughts toward that. Amen.

Praying for Future Relatives

When I was a teenager, my grandmother told me that she had been praying for my spouse-to-be from the day I was born. I wasn't engaged when she confessed this to me. I hadn't even met Mike yet. But Grandma knew he was out there, so she prayed for him and for his family. I can't remember if she prayed for our children then, too, or not, but it wouldn't surprise me to learn that she did.

Knowing that Grandma was praying for people she hadn't met and that I, at the time, wasn't even sure existed, made quite an impression on me. I've tried to follow her example, anticipating the people who might come into our lives and praying for them *now* — friends, mentors, spouses, grandchildren. God knows who they are and what they'll need and how they'll influence our lives and how we'll impact them. When I pray about all this, I entrust our future to Him.

Even more amazing is knowing that Grandma prayed for future family members who didn't show up until after she'd moved on into eternity. If we follow her example, we can pray not only for family we'll probably get to meet but also for the future of our entire family line. I can't see that far. I will not live to see that far. But I can pray right now that God will be with these precious people every step of the way through whatever they *will* encounter throughout their amazing lives.

Father, thank You for a grandmother who prayed about the future and for people who would enter my life. Remind me often to do the same. Amen.

Praying for the Future of Society

In the previous prayer, I encouraged you to pray for future relatives, even those you may never meet. We can do this because prayers don't expire when we die. God continues to work faithfully in the lives of people on earth even after those who've prayed for them have joined Him in Heaven. We pray with hope for the future answers to our prayers on behalf of our loved ones, exercising faith in God's ability to answer in His timing whether we're there to see it or not.

We see this in practice throughout the Bible, most notably from Jesus Himself in John 17. But we also see it practiced in our own history. Before the Civil War, slaves gathered in secret to pray for freedom. They didn't believe that slavery would end in their lifetime, but they *did* have hope for their children and grandchildren. For these they prayed. God answered those prayers.

During World War II, Christians who recognized the evil taking place and growing stronger in Germany prayed against it. Many didn't survive the Holocaust, yet God answered their prayers. We can follow these examples.

When we see negative influences and practices and beliefs in society *now*, we can pray that God will abolish them. They may seem deeply entrenched, yet we can pray that God will open people's eyes to subtle forms of evil, so that they can stop it in order to make life better for the next generation or two or three or four or one hundred!

Rather than complain about the direction we fear society is headed in, let's choose to pray with faith. For our children, grandchildren, great-grandchildren and more, let's pray for the people God will bring into their lives—spouses, friends, and such. Let's pray for the society they'll live in. Let's pray against the evil influences of this world. Let's follow the example of Jesus found in John 17:

> "My prayer is not for them alone. I pray also for those who will believe in me through their message, that all of them may be one, Father, just as you are in me and I am in you. May they also be in us so that the world may believe that you have sent me. I have given them the glory that you gave me, that they may be one as we are one—I in them and you in me—so that they may be brought

to complete unity. Then the world will know that you sent me and have loved them even as you have loved me" (verses 20-23).

Father, when what see hear and see causes us concern about our society, please remind us to pray. Amen.

Praying for People to Reach Their Potential in Christ

One Spring in my then-new backyard, I discovered a few Iris plants with buds getting ready to bloom. I was so excited that I took my camera outside every day, anticipating beautiful flowers to photograph.

Sadly, a storm hit before the flowers opened up, causing them to shrivel where they grew. I didn't get to enjoy those beautiful flowers that year. But I did learn a new *Parachute Prayer,* a prayer for potential.

Whenever we see a flower getting ready to bloom, let's pray for those people we know who are on the brink of such a bloom themselves. These people could include children, high school and college students, people embarking on new careers or entering a new phase of life–the empty nest, a relocation, or retirement. We can also pray for newborn Christians discovering what it means to live for Jesus and discovering His purposes for their lives.

Life is fragile and unpredictable, after all. Each person's salvation is what matters most of all. Yet God has plans for each person's life. Let's ask God to give each person all he or she needs to mature, bloom fully, and bring glory to His name.

Father, thank You for Your care and provision. You have a plan, but You've given us freedom of choice. Sometimes, we admit, our choices — or the choices of others — keep us from becoming all You've meant for us to be. To help prevent this in the lives of people we love, remind us to pray often for potential to be reached. Provide all that our loved ones need to become the people You mean for them to be, then help them to use those resources to the best advantage. Amen.

Praying in Agreement with Loved Ones

For this *Parachute Prayer*, we'll need to stop and think about our Christian ancestors. Let's ask ourselves: What and who were they praying for? And have their prayers been answered? If not, let's add ours to theirs.

I've already noted in a previous *Parachute Prayer* that our ancestors' prayers haven't expired — God is still working to bring the answers about, so that's not why we add our prayers to theirs. But we know there is strength in numbers when people pray. Therefore, we can agree with our ancestors in prayer, joining hands with them, so to speak, just as we join hands with fellow believers for current concerns.

Time is a human thing, and God exists outside of it. I can't even begin to fathom or explain how that works. (C.S. Lewis and George MacDonald both tried.) I know what it means, though, regarding this prayer. When I pray for something that my ancestors prayed for, it's as if we're all praying together, all at the same time — doesn't that just boggle your mind?!

Let me put this in simpler terms. If I know my great-grandmother prayed that all of her descendants would come to follow Christ *and* I know that some of her descendants are *not yet* following Christ, I can remind God of my great-grandmother's prayer then pray for the specific people it now concerns. I strengthen her prayer with knowledge and details that she didn't have. I also find comfort and strength for myself, knowing Great-Grandma prayed for the same people I'm now praying for.

Joining with the past and looking to the future, let's pray for all that we can *now*. To make this a true *Parachute Prayer*, let's give ourselves a simple reminder to pray. Whenever you come across a treasured family heirloom, take time to remember your ancestors and pause to agree with their prayers.

Father, my ancestors cared about their descendants — even those they knew they would never meet. I understand this, because I care about my descendants, too. Please put things in motion now to impact them at just the right time. Draw them into Your kingdom while they are still young. Please bring all of my relatives to Christ. Amen.

Thanking God for What We Overlook

One year as I watched the new ladies' figure skating champion take the ice for her celebration performance, commentators told us that she was skating to thank all who supported her — even the ice!

"She's thanking the ice!" I thought that was strange. Then I realized that without the ice, there'd be no figure skating. How tragic would *that* be?! I thanked God for ice right there.

Today's *Parachute Prayer* is to follow this skater's example and thank God for all the things we can think of that we need but overlook. As we move through our day, let's try to not take anything for granted. What supports us so that we can be the people God created us to be?

Cleaning house, for example, is a never-ending battle to get rid of dirt. Yet dirt allows plants to grow which create the oxygen we breathe. It also provides a ground for us to walk on over the earth's molten insides. I think, perhaps, we need to thank God for dirt — even as we work to keep it where it belongs — outside.

Which reminds us to thank God for that work. Meaningful work gives our lives purpose, builds self-esteem, and allows us to serve God and others every day.

And as each work-filled day ends, we thank God for night and time to sleep. Sometimes I long to stay awake, to accomplish more, to experience more of life. Without sleep, though, I'd be too exhausted to accomplish or experience much of anything. Besides, nothing feels better after a long and busy day than a just-right mattress and cozy blankets to wrap oneself up in.

Father, we thank You for ice and dirt and work and night and sleep — and for everything else we need but take for granted. Help us to notice what You provide and thank You every day! Amen.

Praying for the People Who Matter Most to You

I think it's easy to intercede for the people in our lives. When we see their needs, our hearts go out to them and we're compelled to pray. It's also easy to pray about struggles or concerns within relationships. We long for perfect peace and unity and know that only God can fully bring it about. We eagerly ask God for wisdom and grace — and pray He'll give it to our loved ones, too.

But how often do we just sit, reflect, and thank God for each of the precious people in our lives? How often do we remember the things they've done to bless our lives? How often do we reflect on what their blessed existence means to us personally? How often do we go before God's throne to pray,

> "Father, this person is amazing! You blessed the world when you put him (or her) in it. I am a better person for knowing this one. Thank you, my providential Lord!"?

Consider the following verses: "We always thank God for all of you and continually mention you in our prayers. We remember before our God and Father your work produced by faith, your labor prompted by love, and your endurance inspired by hope in our Lord Jesus Christ." —1 Thessalonians 1:2-3. Paul and his companions thanked God for the Thessalonians. They reminded God of what those people had done. (God didn't need the reminder, but He's pleased when we notice what His other children do.) They cited fruit of the Spirit obviously growing in the Thessalonian church—faith, love, endurance (long-suffering, patience). And, most important of all, they gave Christ all the glory for His work through them.

Little children often pray, "God bless Mommy and Daddy and Sister and Brother and Grandpa and Grandma and the dog and the cat" and so on and so forth attempting to name every person (and animal) they've ever met. Maybe we should follow their example sometimes, lingering in God's presence, thanking Him specifically for the many people who daily bless our lives.

Father, thank you for those who've chosen to read this Parachute Prayer *today. I am so blessed to be able to share these thoughts with them. Bless them abundantly as they go on about their day. They're precious to You — that makes them precious to me. Amen.*

Praying for People of Other Places

Today's *Parachute Prayer* is simple: when you see pictures of famous landmarks, pray for the people of the city or country the landmark is located in. Pictures may be on-line, on television, or used as décor in an office or home. You might even see a landmark in person if you are traveling.

If you live near such a landmark, it can remind you to pray for your hometown. If you see a picture of the Eiffel Tower, pray for people who live in Paris or maybe all of France. If you see a picture of the Gateway Arch, pray for the people of St. Louis, Missouri.

This *Parachute Prayer* might tie in with praying the day's headlines. If you see the landmark in the news because of something happening in that city, you'll know exactly what to pray about. But we know there are needs in every city, every country, whether these make the news or not. And God knows what these needs are. When we recognize a famous landmark, let's take a moment to pray.

Father, help us to remember that people all over the world have problems and cares. Remind us to pray about these, and inspire our prayers that we'll cover even unknown needs. Amen.

Praying for Unspoken Requests

Today's prayer is for the silent or unspoken request. I'm not talking about the "unspoken" request often mentioned in prayer meetings, though we should take those seriously, too. It just occurs to me that a lot of people carry their burdens all alone. God hears, honors, and answers their prayers, yet what a privilege to share the load when we can.

When someone we know seems especially quiet or down, that's a cue to offer a prayer. Yet some with deep concerns will never let on at all. To pray for these, whenever you're feeling especially quiet or down, ask God's Spirit to bring names and faces to mind of people for whom He'd like you to pray. When He does this, and He will, pray for these people's unspoken concerns.

Father, sometimes people just don't feel like sharing their concerns. We'd like to pray for them anyway. In our quiet moments, please bring names and faces to our minds. For these people we will pray. Amen.

Praying for Others as We Pray for Ourselves

I once read that Charles Spurgeon, a great Christian minister known for his amazing sermons, had an interesting practice of giving. It was simple. Whenever he bought something other than a necessity for himself, he'd give an equal amount of money to someone else. For example, if he bought a book for himself with a cost of $13.00, he'd donate another $13.00 to charity. The purpose of the practice was to keep him from spending too much on himself while helping him remember to give generously to people in need.

Today, I'd like to suggest we turn the concept into a *Parachute Prayer*. Whenever we pray for ourselves, let's take a little extra time to pray the same for someone else. For instance, if we're praying about a personal health concern, let's remember others with related concerns. If we're praying about a financial need, let's pray for people we know who are struggling financially. If we're asking God to give us something or to help us solve a problem, let's ask Him to do the same for someone else. If we're praying for parenting wisdom, let's pray for friends with kids.

God wants us to ask Him for the things we want and need. He also wants us to trust His wisdom in answering yes or no. He is our loving Father, Creator, and Provider. We show our confidence in Him when we take our concerns and desires to Him daily. But as we do, let's take the concerns and desires of others to Him, too.

Father, Jesus taught us to pray, "Give us this day our daily bread." And so, we bring our daily requests to You, knowing You will provide generously and with our best interests in mind. As we trust You for the concerns of our own lives, please remind us to entrust You with the cares of others, too. You have more than enough for all of us. Thank You for Your love above all. Amen.

Recognizing a Call to Worship

I don't know what the weather's like around your house right now, but it's been kind of a gloomy day around here. I've opened all the windows to let the sunshine in, but there isn't any to be found. Even the dog is sulking. He likes to lie in the sunny spot on the floor. I giggle whenever he has to move to stay in the sunshine as that spot moves over the course of a usual day.

There's no sunny spot today.

But there is a gentle breeze. I can see it rustling the leaves of trees and bushes around our house. Sometimes it gets a little more aggressive, causing colorful leaves to dance, then fall. Pleasant to watch — even on a non-sunshiny day.

Psalm 89:15-16 says, "Happy are those who hear the joyful call to worship, for they will walk in the light of your presence, LORD. They rejoice all day long in your wonderful reputation. They exult in your righteousness" (NLT). Reflecting on these verses led me to think of walking in the light of God's presence. He's with us all the time every day. But sometimes we forget.

The Psalmist says those who hear the joyful call to worship are happy, rejoicing all day long in God's wonderful reputation, exulting in His righteousness. That call to worship is available to everyone! Yet, not everyone hears it. Why? It's something we have to want to hear. It's something we have to train ourselves to recognize.

Thankfully, the God of All Creation has given something to help us with this. When we see the sunshine crawling across our floors or feel its warmth on our skin, let's let it remind us that God is here. He's not in the sunshine, but He created it. Let's let it be our call to worship Him.

Likewise, when we see the leaves dancing and beginning to fall or feel the crisp, cool Autumn air, let's let these do the same. Let's recognize the sunshine and the breeze as gifts from their Creator to us, gifts that can call us to express our thanksgiving and praise.

Father, I want to walk in the light of Your presence every day — and be aware of it as I do! Thank You for simple reminders that You are everywhere, that You created everything, that I can stop and talk to You anytime, about anything. I love You, Lord! Amen.

223

Praying for Our Circles

In his book, *Prayer: Finding the Heart's True Home,* Richard Foster says, "We are responsible before God to pray for those God brings into our circle of nearness." This pretty much means that we are to pray for the people God brings into our lives. We're to pray for the people we come into contact with daily, the people we communicate with often over distance, the people we hear about who need to be remembered in prayer.

And don't we *all* need to be remembered in prayer?

That thought aside, my imagination went to work when I read Foster's words. I pictured myself sitting on a park bench in the center of a circle that only I could see, quietly praying for each person who just happened to be located within that space.

I'm not sure that that's what Foster had in mind when he said we're responsible to pray for everyone God brings into our circle of nearness, but I do know it's how some of my *Parachute Prayers* work: praying for everyone in the doctor's office or grocery check-out line as we wait, praying for children we see walking to or from school, praying for people who happen to come to our door or call on the phone. Our circles of nearness can be defined in many ways.

To remember this concept and our responsibility, let's use circles as our cue. Whenever we see circles, let's pause to pray for the people who are in our circles, whether we're praying for our family circle, our circle of friends, a *Google+* circle we belong to, or everyone who happens to be standing in an imaginary circle we draw with our minds wherever we happen to be.

Father, remind us often of our responsibility to pray for the people You bring into our lives. And please find us faithful for their good, for Your glory, and for our growth. Amen.

Conclusion:
The Four Blessings of *Parachute Prayer*

As with all kinds of prayer, *Parachute Prayers* don't only bless the people we are praying for. Prayer, after all, is the privilege we have of talking with God. Whenever we take time to do this, whether for a determined length of time or through a quickly whispered prayer, God is delighted to hear our voices or thoughts specifically directed His way. We will be blessed through the activity.

Here are just a few ways God will bless us through the practice of *Parachute Prayer:*

1. Parachute Prayers *Remind Us of God's Presence All the Time*

As we add prompts for *Parachute Prayers* to our repertoire, we'll gradually gain a greater awareness of God's presence in our lives and throughout our world. Breathing sentence prayers throughout the day, wherever we are, whatever we are doing, and about anything and everything, will remind us as we do that God is here.

An awareness of God's presence is crucial to maturing spiritual life. If we're facing a crisis, this knowledge will prompt us to call on Him for strength in a moment instead of relying on our own—which can be disastrous. When temptation tries to draw us into sin's lair, knowing God is with us can help us to resist. Even the beautiful moments of life are enhanced when we think of God and thank Him for such gifts.

2. Parachute Prayers *Remind Us to Talk to Our God*

Ephesians 6:18 tells us to "pray in the Spirit on all occasions with all kinds of prayers and requests." To me this means that God wants us to talk to Him about anything and everything. *Parachute Prayers* can remind us to do this.

If a friend came to visit, you wouldn't sit her on the couch in your living room and go on about your business as if she weren't there. No — you'd either sit down beside her and visit for a while or invite her to join you in your day's activities.

If we think of God in this way, remembering that He is with us all the time, we'll want to talk with Him as we go about each day. Sometimes we'll sit down to visit for a while. Sometimes our conversations will be more businesslike or intense. Sometimes we'll just chat about random subjects that come to mind — most likely prompted by His Spirit — as we do the laundry or run errands. God is the friend who is always with us. He wants us to talk with Him.

3. Parachute Prayers *Help Us Keep Our People and Our World before God All the Time*

The second half of Ephesians 6:18 says, "With this in mind be alert and always keep on praying for all the Lord's people." *Parachute Prayers* teach us to be alert. Just as the Christian songs on the radio reminded me to pray for my son, each prompt in this book will remind us to worship, praise, thank, confess, present a request, or intercede whenever we encounter it in daily life. As you practice some of these ideas, you'll develop more of your own, specific to your life and community. Prayer makes a difference in this world and in people's lives. When we truly believe this, we'll want to remember to pray all the time.

4. Parachute Prayers *Help Us in Our More Focused Prayer Times*

As I mentioned in my second point, there are many kinds of prayer. *Parachute Prayers* are a beneficial means of praying continually, but they shouldn't be the only way we choose to talk to God. Sometimes, daily, in fact, we need to make time to sit down (or kneel or bow) with the express purpose of communicating with God. He is our Father. He loves us. He wants to hear our praises, offerings of thanksgiving, confessions of sin, and prayer requests, both for ourselves and for the people we love. He also wants to communicate His truth to us.

This kind of prayer is not the subject of this book, but *Parachute Prayers* can begin to lead us into it. When we settle down for our more focused times of prayer, God's Spirit will bring subjects for conversation into our mind. We may already have a list of concerns to lay at God's feet, but if we've been praying throughout the day about things we've done or people we've seen, God's Spirit may bring these back to our minds for a more lengthy discussion. He may prompt us to intercede for someone. He may remind us of a service opportunity and call us to action. Whatever catches our attention through a *Parachute Prayer* reminder, prompting a quick and immediate prayer, may become a more lengthy prayer concern as we approach our God later in a more focused prayer.

Father, please call us to pray often. Remind us of Your presence, that You are with us all the time. And as we remember this, remind us to talk to You about whatever is on our minds. Train us to watch for opportunities to keep our people and our world before You in prayer both as we go about our daily activities and in the times we set aside specifically to pray. Lord, we want to know You better, and we want our loved ones to know You, too. Please teach us to pray. Amen.

Acknowledgments

Father, I thank You for inviting us to pray. I thank You, also, for listening. You hear. You care. You love. You created life, and Your presence makes it worth living. For both, I thank You!

Mike, my dear husband, your confidence in me keeps me going when I lose it in myself. Sometimes I think you dream for the both of us! Thank You for sharing life with me.

Justin, Alex, and Seth: there's nothing like a son to teach a mom to pray—and that is a good thing for all of us! I am so thankful God chose to place each of you in our family. Thank You for letting Him teach you and bring each of you peace (Isaiah 54:13).

Alex, I thank you especially for graciously agreeing to let me to include your part in this book's history. You are *Beloved*. Keep growing in God, Son.

Precious Women Of the Chapel wherever I've been blessed to speak, thank you for letting God teach you to pray *Parachute Prayers* and for encouraging me with your stories of such—days, weeks, months, and more later. Let's keep practicing together, growing closer to our Lord.

Janet Benlien Reeves is an Army chaplain's wife, an empty-nest mom, and the author of *Home Is Where God Sends You: Lessons in Contentment from Nearby and Faraway.* She holds a bachelor's degree in Christian education from Point Loma Nazarene University. In between moves and visits to family scattered all over the United States, she enjoys reading, writing, running, and flower hunting. Janet and her husband have three grown sons, a precious daughter-in-law, and a senior citizen dog who still thinks he is a puppy.

Visit Janet at her website: *WildflowerFaith.com.*

www.ingramcontent.com/pod-product-compliance
Lightning Source LLC
LaVergne TN
LVHW051114080426
835510LV00018B/2036